TORO Expert Guide to

LAWNS

PRO SECRETS FOR A BEAUTIFUL YARD

CRE▲TIVE
HOMEOWNER®

 Expert Guide to

LAWNS

PRO SECRETS FOR A BEAUTIFUL YARD

JOSEPH R. PROVEY
KRIS ROBINSON
with VAN CLINE, PhD

CREATIVE HOMEOWNER®, Upper Saddle River, New Jersey

Toro Expert Guide to Lawns
Produced by Home & Garden Editorial Services
Authors: Joe Provey, Kris Robinson
Contributor: Roy Barnhart
Consultants: Van Cline, PhD, Cathy Beauregard
Layout and Design: Venera Alexandrova, Horst Weber
Copy Editor: Owen Lockwood
Editorial Assistant: MaryAnn Kopp
Photo Prepress: Carl Weese
Illustrations: Vincent Alessi (computer-generated site plans), Todd Ferris (tool and equipment paintings), Wendy Smith Griswald (structural concept paintings)
Front Cover Photography: Barry L. Runk
Inside Front Cover Photography: Janet Loughrey Photography
Back Cover Photography: *Top* Lefever/Grushow; *bottom* Joe Provey/Carl Weese
Inside Back Cover Photography: *From top to bottom* Carl Weese; Carl Weese; Courtesy of Toro; Robert Perron

Creative Homeowner
Vice President, Publisher: Timothy O. Bakke
Production Director: Kimberly H. Vivas
Art Director: David Geer
Managing Editor: Fran Donegan
Digital Imaging Specialist: Frank Dyer
Editorial Assistant: Nora Grace

Toro Expert Guide to Lawns, First Edition
First published as *Better Lawns, Step by Step*
Library of Congress Control Number: 2007932960
ISBN-10: 1-58011-375-3
ISBN-13: 978-1-58011-375-5

Current Printing (last digit)
10 9 8 7 6 5 4 3 2 1

CREATIVE HOMEOWNER®
A Division of Federal Marketing Corp.
24 Park Way
Upper Saddle River, NJ 07458
www.creativehomeowner.com

Acknowledgments

Many thanks to Pete Robinson, Priscilla Williams, Roy Barnhart, Carl Weese, and Cathy Beauregard for helping to make this book possible. Special thanks to The Toro Company for sharing its knowledge about growing and maintaining great lawns.

CONTENTS

The Allure of Lawns

The lawn has been the most powerful landscaping tradition in North America for more than a century. Anthropologists suggest that the reason is genetic. People feel more comfortable surrounded by the savanna-like expanses that were home to the ancestors from whom we've evolved. Sociologists say that manicured green turf is a symbol of peace and order. Historians trace the origins of the modern lawn to eighteenth-century England and France, where lawns became symbols of pride, power, and wealth.

Veteran gardeners offer a more pragmatic explanation for the popularity of lawns. They point out that lawns cover the most ground with the least effort and expense. They also take less time and expertise to grow and maintain than gardens. Surveys back this up. They show that flower and vegetable gardens require upwards of 20 hours of tending per season per 100 square feet. Lawns demand less than an hour of labor per 100 square feet per season.

Those who prefer simple explanations argue that it would be hard to come up with an alternative surface that is as beautiful and functional. Velvet green lawns open views to your house and gardens. They take on a glow from a rising or setting sun that can make you feel that all is right with the world. And there's no better surface upon which to kick a ball or have a picnic. The lawn is a multipurpose surface that can be a badminton court one moment and a water park the next, complete with wading pools and water slides.

George Washington's Mount Vernon estate and Thomas Jefferson's Monticello, above, helped make lawns popular in the United States. Early lawns were maintained with scythes, below.

A Sensible Approach to Lawn Care

While North Americans continue their love affair with the lawn, they are looking for new ways to fit lawn care into their busy lifestyles. The traditional high-maintenance method, with five or six applications of fertilizer, herbicides, and pesticides every year, is no longer an option for many homeowners. Lawn-care services are not right for everyone either, especially for those who are uncomfortable with applying chemicals that may prove hazardous. Health-conscious homeowners don't want to lose control over what goes on their lawns or risk contributing to lawn-related pollution. Instead, smart homeowners are seeking and adopting a new approach: lawn care that's low maintenance and sustainable without worries about family health or environmental pollution.

In *Toro Expert Guide to Lawns*, you'll learn how to have a good-looking lawn with no worries. You'll receive step-by-step directions on restoring an old lawn or replanting a new one with improved grass varieties that require less maintenance. You'll be introduced to the latest in mowing equipment, irrigation techniques that save water, time-saving mowing methods, and ways to control weeds and pests without harmful chemicals.

America is changing the way it thinks about lawns. Homeowners are beginning to understand that the lawn is not a chemistry experiment in which you add the right ingredients and, presto, you have lawn. It turns out growing grass is like growing other plants—get the culture or conditions right, and nature will help you take care of the rest. The lawn remains an important symbol and a key part to creating a modern, functional, and beautiful landscape, but fewer and fewer homeowners want the expensive, labor-intensive, and pollution-generating lawn of the past.

● ●

Did You Know?

England is probably where George Washington fell for lawns. But because using an army of scythe-wielding laborers was too costly, he relied on deer to keep his lawn at Mount Vernon "mowed." Thomas Jefferson, minister to the French Court from 1784 to 1789 and a tourist in England during this period, also brought back many ideas about plants and landscaping, including the idea of building his classical estate, Monticello, on a vast lawn.

PART 1

REVIVING YOUR LAWN

Assessing Your Lawn's Design

You can become accustomed to nearly anything: door latches that don't catch, windows that don't open, stairs that squeak. That's true in the case of a lawn, too. You pass by it every day and even mow it for years without really thinking about it. But does it look as good as it could? Is there too much of it? Not enough? Does it cost more to maintain than it needs to? The "Lawn Design" score sheet on page 16 will help you assess the strengths and flaws of your lawn's design. It will help you think about how your lawn should look and function. Then you'll be able to turn a critical eye on your lawn and redesign it with a pencil and paper. If your lawn design passes the test or if you're happy with the way your lawn is laid out now, you may skip the rest of this chapter and turn to Chapter 2, "Rating Your Lawn's Condition," on page 28.

Ground-level edging allows you to mow without needing to raise your mower blade or return later with a trimmer.

Design a Lawn for Your Lifestyle

Today's lawn is required to host an ever-growing variety of outdoor activities. No longer is it just a simple game of catch. Soccer, lacrosse, volleyball, and touch football are demanding on residential properties and require more rugged turf than today's conventional lawns. Similarly, backyard entertaining is on the upswing. Why fight traffic and crowds when you can have everything in your own backyard "resort"? Pools, spas, and even outdoor kitchens are being installed in record setting numbers. And it all means more challenges and opportunities for people with lawns.

The first step in redesigning your lawn is to list all the ways you use your yard. Be sure to include projections of your future needs. Don't be concerned if your list is long. Refer to the "Yard Activities Checklist" on

(Continued on page 18.)

A well-designed lawn, above and below, not only provides play and picnic areas but also shows off your gardens and the surrounding landscape.

Yard Activities Checklist

Welcoming guests

Chatting with neighbors

Storing firewood, trash, toys, etc.

Drying clothes

Walking and exercising pets

Strolling around the yard

Flower gardening

Vegetable gardening

Enjoying backyard sports

Providing water activities for children

Sunbathing

Bird watching

Entertaining family and friends

Cooking and eating outdoors

Playing with playhouses or swing sets

Parking off-street

Other

The curved lines of this lawn give it a natural feel. Garden mulch and a well-defined edge, however, help keep maintenance to a minimum.

SCORE SHEET

Lawn Design

Rate your lawn's design by placing a check next to the statements that best describe it. When you're done, add up your total points, and match that total to the Score Guide below.

Score Guide

26–30 Congratulations! You have a well-designed lawn.

20–25 You have a fairly well-designed lawn, but you should consider making minor design improvements.

15–19 You have an old-fashioned lawn of the 1950s and should plan to redesign. You don't need to do it all at once, but now is the time to get started.

10–14 Your lawn design is a disaster! Use the design tips provided in this chapter, or call in a professional landscape designer to help you create a better design.

Size of Lawn

❑ (3 pts.) Your lawn and nonlawn areas (patios, pools, gardens, ground covers, woods, etc.) are balanced.

❑ (2 pts.) Your lawn is either too big or too small for your needs.

❑ (1 pt.) Your lawn is too big for you to handle.

Shape of Lawn

❑ (3 pts.) Your lawn areas complement the design of your house and garden beds.

❑ (2 pts.) Your lawn areas are laid out in pleasing shapes, but they don't enhance your house or gardens.

❑ (1 pt.) Your lawn is a series of big rectangles bordered by rows of garden beds and shrubs that don't relate well to your house.

Drainage

❑ (3 pts.) Rain is absorbed by your lawn, and it rarely runs off into storm sewers, ponds, or streams—even after a heavy rain.

❑ (2 pts.) Your lawn has several areas of bare soil due to erosion, especially near downspouts; rain sometimes runs into

your basement or to the street.

❑ (1 pt.) In addition to basement or street runoff problems, you have standing water on your lawn after rainstorms.

Ease of Maintenance

❑ (3 pts.) Your lawn is easy to mow, irrigate and fertilize; it's also fairly level, and there are few mowing obstacles.

❑ (2 pts.) In order to complete mowing, you have to make many tight turns, mow close to tree trunks, bend down under low-hanging branches, or move lawn furniture. You need several hundred feet of hose to irrigate your lawn.

❑ (1 pt.) You frequently need to traverse steep slopes to mow your lawn, or you need to walk your mower through garden beds to get to other parts of the yard. As a result, you find yourself wasting time by mowing the same lawn strips two or three times. Your irrigation plan amounts to praying regularly for rain.

Edge Treatments

❑ (3 pts.) A grass-free border around the edges of your lawn keeps grass from spreading into your beds and

Lawns have several beneficial effects on the local environment, including natural cooling, oxygen production, and airborne particulate control.

Did You Know? In a typical 1,000 square feet of lawn, there are about 1 million grass plants. Just 625 square feet of grass supplies all of the oxygen a person needs for one day.

makes edge trimming with a mower quick and easy.

❏ (2 pts.) You've invested in landscape ties or plastic or steel edging, and the lawn's edges are tidy but require more than 30 minutes of hand- or power-trimming every week.

❏ (1 pt.) The edges between your garden beds and lawn are ragged or nonexistent and are breeding grounds for weeds.

Proportion and Scale

❏ (3 pts.) The lawn is an important element of your landscape design, but it does not dominate the property.

❏ (2 pts.) The trees and shrubs in your lawn are dotted at random around the property, not in groups or with other plants. They look lonely, as though someone told them to wait there and then never returned.

❏ (1 pt.) Your house and your garden beds seem lost in a sea of green.

Grass Selection

❏ (3 pts.) Your lawn turf is dense, with a consistent deep-green color and lush texture.

❏ (2 pts.) There are a few bare or weedy patches where kids play games or use play equipment.

❏ (1 pt.) Your lawn has a two-tone appearance, brown and green, for extended periods.

Traffic and Circulation

❏ (3 pts.) The entrances to your lawn are wide, and you've installed pathways or hardscaping wherever frequent foot traffic is unavoidable.

❏ (2 pts.) Your lawn design forces walkers to tread upon the same areas repeatedly, resulting in some bare spots.

❏ (1 pt.) Years of parking vehicles on your lawn and treading the same routes have worn ruts and bare dirt paths.

Views

❏ (3 pts.) Your lawn provides many attractive vistas as the seasons change, from inside your house and from many vantages around your property.

❏ (2 pts.) Your lawn looks good from most vantage points—the windows you frequently look out of, from outdoor entertainment areas, and from your driveway.

❏ (1 pt.) Your lawn looks good only from the street.

Labor

❏ (3 pts.) You spend one hour or less per week mowing, irrigating, and feeding your lawn.

❏ (2 pts.) You spend between one and two hours per week working on your lawn.

❏ (1 pt.) You spend more than two hours per week, or you have hired a lawn-care service to do most of the work for you.

Cost

❏ (3 pts.) On average, you spend less than $250 on your lawn and lawn equipment per year.

❏ (2 pts.) You spend between $250 and $350 per year.

❏ (1 pt.) You spend more than $350 per year.

To begin your site plan, draw the boundaries of your property and lawn areas. Use a 100-foot tape for taking measures, and write them in on your plan.

(Continued from page 15.)

page 15 to help you along, and then show your list to other family members for their input. Once you have a comprehensive list, prioritize the activities in the order of importance to your family.

Creating a Plan

The next step in redesigning your lawn is to come up with a site plan. If your property is half an acre or less, measure the boundaries, and draw a sketch of the property to scale on a large sheet of paper. When drawing to scale, it's helpful to begin with a grid in which each division equals a given number of feet. If your property is larger than half an acre, measure and sketch only the lawn areas, beginning with a sketch of the front lawn.

If you have a survey of your property or a professionally drawn site plan, you can skip the above. Just copy the site lines on paper on which you can draw.

Step-By-Step Drawings

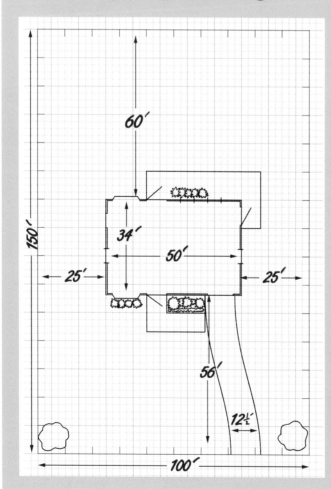

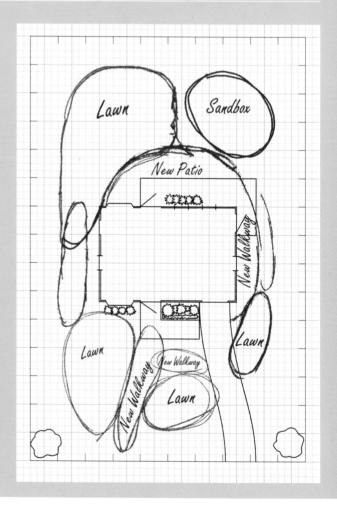

If you don't have a site plan or survey, it may be on file at your local building department, where you can make a copy for a nominal fee.

Once you have the outline of the area you're re-designing, begin to fill in the details. Add the decorative and activity-related lawn areas, footprints of structures (including sheds and garages), areas covered by trees, garden beds, and other features of your yard, such as pools, paths and sidewalks, driveways, and play spaces.

Label the areas that correspond to the high-priority activities in the "Yard Activities Checklist" on page 15. Shade in the approximate area that each activity requires, overlapping those areas that can be used for more than one purpose.

Now you can begin sketching changes. Lay a piece of tracing paper over your existing lawn plan and start to sketch new lawn layouts. You may need to

Smart TIP

CUSHION THE BLOW

Play areas, especially those including play structures and swing sets, should be covered with at least 6 inches of wood chips or pea-gravel to reduce impact should a child fall. The material should extend at least 6 feet from elevated platforms and ladders, and at least double the height of the swing beam or the length of the swing's arc.

Far left ON YOUR SITE PLAN, DRAW IN LAWN AREAS, BUILDINGS, WALKS, DRIVEWAYS, PATIOS, DECKS, FENCES, WALLS, TREES, AND GARDEN BEDS, AS WELL AS THEIR APPROXIMATE DIMENSIONS. IT'S ALSO A GOOD IDEA TO INDICATE LOCATIONS OF UTILITY LINES, SETBACKS, AND SEPTIC TANKS.

Left ON TRACING PAPER, OR ON A PHOTOCOPY OF THE EXISTING SITE PLAN, ROUGHLY DRAW "BUBBLES" TO INDICATE WHERE PLANNED AREAS WILL GO. IN THE EXAMPLE, THERE'S A PLACE FOR NEW WALKWAYS, A PATIO, AND A SANDBOX. MAKE SEVERAL PHOTOCOPIES OF THE SITE PLAN AND TRY SEVERAL YARD LAYOUTS BEFORE CHOOSING THE ONE THAT BEST SUITS YOUR NEEDS.

Right FILL LEFTOVER AREAS WITH LOW-MAINTENANCE PLANTINGS, SUCH AS GROUND COVERS AND MULCHED TREES AND SHRUBS. IF YOU WANT TO SAVE WORK BUT STILL WANT FLOWER BEDS, ADD LOW-MAINTENANCE PERENNIALS AND ANNUALS RECOMMENDED BY A LOCAL NURSERY. ALSO, ADD LOW-MAINTENANCE HARDSCAPING, SUCH AS WALKWAYS AND A PATIO.

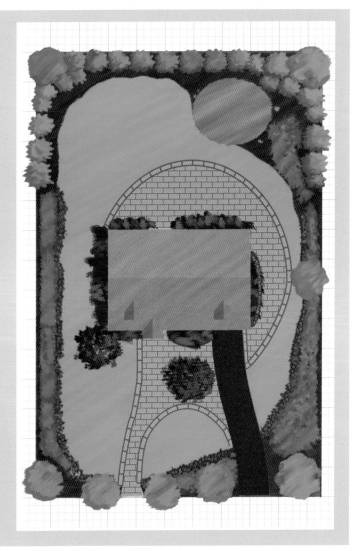

Smart TIP

PLAY BALL!

When redesigning a lawn, leave areas large enough to accommodate the recreational activities you and your family enjoy. For example, an official badminton court measures 20 x 44 feet and requires a total of 30 x 54 feet of lawn. A volleyball court is 30 x 60 feet and requires a total of 50 x 80 feet of space. Croquet, soccer, and touch football can also be accommodated in a 50 x 80-foot area.

use and discard several pieces of tracing paper before you hit upon a layout that begins to look right.

Not sure where to start? Try comparing the amount of lawn you currently maintain with the amount required to support the yard activities you enjoy.

If you have young children, play areas of 3,000 to 5,000 square feet of lawn are probably adequate. But don't go overboard with flower and vegetable gardens. Gardens generally cost more to create and maintain per square foot than lawns, and they are more labor

The redesigned yard HAS EASIER-TO-MAINTAIN BORDERS AND LESS LAWN AREA, AND IT WILL REQUIRE LESS LAWN MAINTENANCE. THERE IS STILL, HOWEVER, PLENTY OF PLAY SPACE FOR KIDS. MASONRY WALKS PREVENT BARE SPOTS DUE TO TRAFFIC. PROPERTY BOUNDARIES ARE WELL DEFINED, AND THE LAWN'S CONTOURS SOFTEN THE HARD LINES OF THE HOUSE.

intensive. On the other hand, islands planted with trees, shrubs, and ground cover, or covered with mulch, are less labor intensive than lawn and in time will cost less to maintain. Take a long look at the lawn areas remaining on your plan. Remember that a primary function of the lawn is to connect the various areas of your yard, giving it a cohesive look and allowing you free access from one area to another. Look for logical ways to connect the lawn areas to each other and to existing paths and driveways. Connections between lawn areas should be at least 10 feet wide to ease mowing and to prevent funneling of foot and equipment traffic to a narrow area. For the same reason, entrances to your lawn from roads, driveways, patios, and decks should also be at least 10 feet wide. Widen the access ways to your lawn if necessary.

More Design Considerations

A good lawn design can help you save money and conserve water. It will also add value to your property and reduce lawn maintenance and pollution. Here are several design goals and suggestions to consider for your plan:

Prevent water runoff. Locate garden beds so that they intercept and absorb runoff from roofs, from driveways, and from elevated lawn areas during heavy rainstorms—or when you let the sprinkler run too long! Doing so will help you avoid sending water and fertilizer runoff into the street and down storm drains. Or create a rain garden to accommodate the runoff.

Eliminate lawn beside streams and around ponds. Create buffer strips of natural vegetation, or plant these strips with noninvasive species appropriate to your region; then mulch. The idea is to prevent soil and runoff from getting into open water. Call a Cooperative Extension Service for a list of plants suited to your area. Many towns and municipalities have published lists and require permits for planting in and around wetlands. Check with your town before you plant, as unwanted invasive species, no matter how beautiful, can choke out the native wildflowers and regional plants that once grew in our woodlands."

Assess existing sprinkler systems. Uneven irriga-

(Continued on page 26.)

Design Solutions

Far left A RETAINING WALL IS A GOOD WAY TO DEAL WITH STEEPLY SLOPED PROPERTY. IT HELPS TO PREVENT WATER RUNOFF AND PROVIDES A MORE LEVEL LAWN FOR EASIER, SAFER MOWING.

Left NATIVE STREAMSIDE PLANTS CREATE AN ATTRACTIVE BUFFER BETWEEN LAWN AND STREAM. ACTING LIKE A GIANT SPONGE, THEY HELP PREVENT MOST LAWN RUNOFF (AND FERTILIZER) FROM REACHING OPEN WATER.

Below left INSTALL PERMANENT PATHS WHEREVER FOOT TRAFFIC IS HEAVY. STONE PAVERS PRESERVE LAWN AREAS AND ARE LOW ENOUGH TO MOW RIGHT OVER.

Below WHILE YOU'RE PLANNING A NEW LAWN, CONSIDER OTHER IMPROVEMENTS, SUCH AS ENHANCING SOIL, ADDING GARDEN BEDS, AND INSTALLING AN IN-GROUND IRRIGATION SYSTEM.

▪ *Ring Trees with Mulch*

Mulched tree rings save mowing time and protect your trees from being injured by the mower or string trimmer. In addition, they keep the tree roots cool and moist. Be careful to use proper mulching techniques. Don't pile mulch too high up the trunk. Referred to as volcano mulching, it can stress and eventually smother and kill an otherwise healthy tree. Also, leave a 3-inch space around the root flare of the tree so that the mulch does not touch the tree trunk. For best results with mulched beds, lay down sheets of water-permeable landscape fabric prior to planting. Shredded cedar, hardwood mulch, shells, gravel, and pine are good top mulches. But take note: pine can be a magnet for ants in some areas!

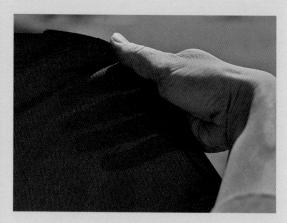

3 TO FIGHT WEEDS, YOU WILL NEED SEVERAL INCHES OF MULCH AND LANDSCAPE FABRIC. CHOOSE FABRIC THAT'S WATER PERMEABLE SO WATER CAN REACH THE TREE ROOTS.

1 MARK THE RING WITH LATEX PAINT. OR USE A HOSE TO MARK THE BORDER.

2 USE A SHARP SPADE TO CUT AN EDGE ALONG THE LINE, BUT AVOID CUTTING THROUGH THE SURFACE ROOTS.

4 CUT LANDSCAPE FABRIC TO THE SHAPE OF THE RING USING SCISSORS, AND THEN MAKE A CUT TO THE CENTER SO THE FABRIC CAN BE PUT AROUND THE TREE TRUNK.

5 COVER WITH 3 IN. OF MULCH. SHREDDED CEDAR, ABOVE, IS A GOOD CHOICE BUT WILL NEED TO BE REPLENISHED REGULARLY.

This well-maintained edge and the mulched woodland garden beyond it help prevent weeds from getting a foothold and spreading to the lawn.

GET AN EDGE

Smart **TIP**

A neat edge looks good and helps to bring a sense of order to your landscape. Ragged, unmaintained borders are breeding grounds for weeds, which can eventually invade the lawn itself. In addition to a simple edge made with a manual or power edger, edges can be made of stone, brick, masonry, wood, metal, or plastic. The best materials allow you to create flat-surface edging, upon which you roll two mower wheels, cutting the lawn edge without needing to raise the mower blade or returning with a string trimmer.

tion patterns because of poor design, neglect, or improper maintenance of a sprinkler system may be wasting water and causing stress in areas of your lawn. Systems that overspray walls, walks, driveways, and streets need to be adjusted. See Chapter 8 for more on lawn irrigation systems.

Don't fight nature. Create planting beds wherever grass is hard to grow—whether because of excessive shade, low-growing trees and shrubs, surface roots, or other inhospitable conditions. Your gardens may contain shrubs, trees, perennials, annuals, and ground covers. Shape the beds to relate to their surroundings, and mulch after planting with 3 to 4 inches of a coarse organic material such as shredded bark or 2 inches of a finer material such as bark chips.

Minimize snow drift. Plant lawn or ground covers beside paths that must be shoveled after snowstorms. Keep the snow off the ground cover, espe-

cially if it is evergreen—piling snow will cause dead spots after the snow melts. Do not plant beds with large woody plants beside paths or build walls or fences there. Snow will drift to the leeward side of such obstructions, making shoveling difficult.

Handle steep slopes. Grass tends to do poorly on steep slopes because it is difficult to establish there and the underlying soil is subject to erosion. Even if you are able to establish good turf, steep slopes can be hazardous to mow. Consider planting a steep slope with ground covers that require little maintenance and help prevent erosion. Another solution is to terrace the slope using materials such as landscape timbers, stone, or masonry.

Install paths. There are three main reasons for installing a path of masonry, stone, or wood in your lawn: improved safety, to show people where you want them to walk (such as to the entry of your home), and to prevent foot traffic from wearing bare

Your lawn underlies your landscape design. Use it to separate and give shape to garden beds. Virtually any tree, shrub, or flower looks better against a lawn.

When planning a lawn with uneven terrain, terraced gardens, above, are a good way to go. In addition, consider the view from key vantage points in your yard as well as inside your home, below.

spots in your turf. When planning your lawn, keep in mind that paths require a lot of trimming and weeding along their boarders and, depending on the design, between the pavers. Where traffic is low, create a path of grass and define the edges with planting beds.

Create privacy, intrigue, and surprise. The secret of successful landscape design is to hold the viewer's attention. Accomplish this not only with dramatic plantings that have interesting texture, foliage, and colorful blooms but also with carefully planned lawn areas. If your yard is big enough, consider creating two or three lawn oases to create "destinations" on your property. Think of them as outdoor rooms, and plan approaches that obscure them until the viewer arrives.

Rating Your Lawn's Condition

Even the most attractively designed lawn will not look good if it's in poor condition. Take a close look at the quality of your lawn, especially in areas that will remain unchanged in your new layout. Is it simply in need of nutrients and more consistent maintenance? Or is it hopelessly infested with weeds and pockmarked with bare spots? Depending on how neglected your lawn has been, you will need to decide whether to restore it or to plant a new one from scratch. Improved maintenance and soil-improving techniques can go a long way toward reviving a tired lawn. But don't waste the time, effort, and expense if the situation is hopeless. How to decide? Survey your lawn for the following problems. Then rate your lawn using the "Rate the Condition of Your Turf" score sheet on page 42.

Soil Types

A soil's ability to sustain grass depends on its type. Clockwise from top left: sandy loam, loamy sand, silt loam, loam, clay loam, humus.

Understanding Soil

Soil is a complex mixture of variously sized particles, water, and air and greatly affects your ability to grow and maintain a beautiful lawn. The particles are mostly mineral fragments generated by the weathering of rocks native to your area. They range in size from sand (0.05 to 2 mm) to silt (0.002 to 0.05 mm) to clay (less than 0.002 mm). Soil texture is determined by the mix of particles. An ideal soil, called loam, has equal amounts of the three types of particles.

When most of the particles in a soil are sand, the soil can be called sand, sandy loam, or loamy sand and may be too porous to retain moisture or nutrients for long. When most of the particles are clay, the soil is known as clay, clay loam, or loamy clay; these "heavy" soils retain too much moisture, and the soil air that grass needs cannot enter the dense clay. When a soil rich in clay dries out, it hardens, and grass roots have a hard time penetrating it. To find out more about the types of soil in your region, call your nearest Cooperative Extension Service.

Soil structure results from soil particles combining to form aggregates. The size, shape, and patterns of these aggregates—ranging from a fine dust to large, blocky soil chunks—also help determine relative proportions of particles, water, and air. Between the aggregates are soil pores, or voids, where grass roots grow, water drains, and small air pockets form. Granular soil, the ideal soil structure for lawns, has pea-size aggregates that are neither too fine nor too large, and a balance of air, moisture-holding ability, and adequate drainage.

Compacted Soil

The greatest enemy of good soil structure in lawns is compaction. Lawn soil often becomes compacted because it takes a pounding: every square foot gets stepped on as we mow, traipse to the shed or woodpile, or romp with pets or kids.

Compaction is detrimental for several reasons. First, compacted soil inhibits root development. Second, air has been squeezed out of the soil, along with the oxygen plant roots need to grow properly. Third, compaction reduces the soil's ability to retain water. Compaction also dramatically reduces the population of essential microorganisms in the soil. These bacteria, fungi, algae, and protozoa prepare nutrients in the soil so that the grass plants can use them.

To assess the degree of soil compaction in your lawn, try pushing a long screwdriver into the turf after a three- or four-day stretch without rain

▪ *Soil Composition*

GRANULAR SOIL, WITH A BALANCE OF AIR, WATER RETENTION, AND DRAINAGE, HELPS GRASS GROW DEEP, STRONG ROOTS.

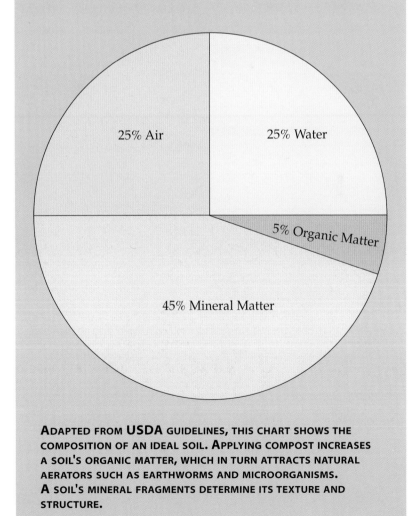

ADAPTED FROM USDA GUIDELINES, THIS CHART SHOWS THE COMPOSITION OF AN IDEAL SOIL. APPLYING COMPOST INCREASES A SOIL'S ORGANIC MATTER, WHICH IN TURN ATTRACTS NATURAL AERATORS SUCH AS EARTHWORMS AND MICROORGANISMS. A SOIL'S MINERAL FRAGMENTS DETERMINE ITS TEXTURE AND STRUCTURE.

Testing for Soil Type

1 A SIMPLE TEST FOR SOIL TYPE IS TO FORM A BALL BY PRESSING THE SOIL BETWEEN YOUR PALMS. (WAIT A DAY OR TWO AFTER WATERING OR RAINFALL TO PERFORM THIS TEST.)

2 BOUNCE THE SOIL BALL A FEW TIMES GENTLY IN YOUR CUPPED HANDS.

3 A BALL THAT CRUMBLES EASILY WITHOUT HOLDING ITS SHAPE CONSISTS MOSTLY OF SAND. ONE THAT STAYS INTACT IS LIKELY MADE OF SILT AND CLAY. IF THE BALL CRUMBLES, AS SHOWN, IT'S LIKELY THAT THE SOIL HAS A GOOD BALANCE OF SAND, SILT, AND CLAY.

4 LASTLY, RUB THE SOIL SAMPLE BETWEEN YOUR FINGERS. A SANDY SOIL WILL FEEL GRITTY. CLAY SOIL WILL FEEL SMOOTH AND SLIPPERY. SILT SOIL WILL FEEL SMOOTH AND SILKY.

or water. If you find it difficult to push the screw-driver in to its handle, your soil is probably compacted. Other signs of lawn soil compaction include the presence of surface roots from nearby trees, excessive weeds, grass with short roots, and a buildup of dead shoot and roots, called thatch, just above the soil surface.

• • • • • • • • • • • • • • • • • • • •

Did You Know? *According to Money magazine, a well-maintained, healthy, attractive lawn can improve the value of a home by up to 15 percent.*

Earthworms are a sign of healthy soil. They not only aerate the soil, bringing oxygen to grass roots, but also produce castings that fertilize and enrich the soil.

Test for soil compaction by pushing a screwdriver into the ground after a period of several days without rain. If it is difficult to penetrate the soil, it will be difficult for grass to thrive, too.

Infertile Soil

Although you should have your soil tested for an accurate reading of its nutrient levels, it's possible to see whether your lawn is getting enough "food" just by taking a close look at it. If the color of your grass is a deep green and the turf is dense, your lawn is in good shape. If the grass is a pale yellowish green and thin, your soil is probably low on nutrients. The presence of crabgrass and plantains probably means that your soil also has fertility problems.

Grass plants need more than a dozen nutrients, but most are required in such small amounts that you don't need to worry about them. Three nutrients, however, are required in relatively large quantities to maintain vigorous grass growth: nitrogen (N), phosphorus (P), and potassium (K).

Nitrogen gives grass a deep green color, promotes dense growth, and helps grass bounce back from injury and wear. With insufficient nitrogen, grass yellows and stops growing. Phosphorus fosters vigorous growth and helps young plants establish strong root systems. Grass deficient in phosphorus may be a reddish purple and will have thin, weak leaves. Potassium increases disease resistance and improves hardiness during periods of high temperature and low moisture. Potassium deficiencies may cause yellow veining on grass blades and browning of blade tips.

Because nitrogen is consumed by plants, lost to the atmosphere, and leached from the soil quickly it should be added periodically. Phosphorus and potassium bind to soil particles and stay in the soil for many years. Except in very sandy soils, they don't need to be replenished frequently.

Too much of any nutrient can be just as harmful as not enough. For example, excessive nitrogen can reduce root growth and make grass vulnerable to disease. Overfertilization is also a major contributor to water pollution because runoff carries it to streams and lakes.

Signs of Infertile Soil

THE TYPES OF WEEDS IN YOUR LAWN CAN GIVE YOU CLUES ABOUT YOUR SOIL'S CONDITION. CRABGRASS, ABOVE LEFT, AND PLANTAINS, ABOVE RIGHT, MAY INDICATE INFERTILITY. BUTTERCUPS, RIGHT, SUGGEST POOR DRAINAGE.

Lack of Humus

You don't need to be a soil scientist to figure out if your soil is deficient in decayed organic matter, or humus. Dig up a sample of the topsoil (top layer) under your lawn. Hold it loosely in your hands and note its color. A pale or light color, especially if the topsoil in your area is typically dark, may mean your soil is lacking in humus—a vital ingredient for a healthy lawn.

You can build up the humus content of your soil by adding compost to it. Adding compost to lawn soil will also help keep soil aerated and thus improve the soil's ability to retain water. In addition, compost supports beneficial microbial life in the soil. For lawn grasses, soil should contain at least 2 percent humus.

To make compost, add equal amounts of materials that are dry and brown with those that are moist and green. Pile the materials loosely into the bin in thin 1- to 3-inch layers, first of brown matter and then of green. Next, add a thin layer of soil (to introduce microbes), and sprinkle the pile with water. Your pile should be about as moist as a wrung-out sponge. Continue to add equal amounts of brown and green and to sprinkle each layer with soil.

When you have 3 feet or so of mixed green and brown matter in your bin, the material will start to break down as a result of the digestive processes of the microbes in the soil layers. You'll know this is happening when the pile starts to heat up inside and eventually shrinks. You can continue to add layers of new materials on top, or you can mix the new materials right into the pile, remembering the half-brown, half-green rule.

Once your bin is full, you have several choices. Let the pile be, and you'll have ready-to-use compost in a year or so. Or you can have ready-to-use compost in as little as a few months if you turn and mix the pile with a garden fork or pitchfork every week or so until its contents are a uniform, crumbly dark brown.

Two Simple Composters

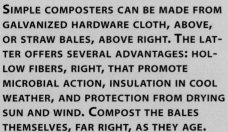

SIMPLE COMPOSTERS CAN BE MADE FROM GALVANIZED HARDWARE CLOTH, ABOVE, OR STRAW BALES, ABOVE RIGHT. THE LATTER OFFERS SEVERAL ADVANTAGES: HOLLOW FIBERS, RIGHT, THAT PROMOTE MICROBIAL ACTION, INSULATION IN COOL WEATHER, AND PROTECTION FROM DRYING SUN AND WIND. COMPOST THE BALES THEMSELVES, FAR RIGHT, AS THEY AGE.

A Three-Bin Composter

With this wooden bin design, you have the option of expanding to three bins—as shown in the illustrations below. Use one bin for fresh kitchen and yard waste, one for decaying material, and one for material that's nearly ready for use.

Smart TIP

BALANCED COMPOST

Depending on the season, you may have more green materials (summer weeds) or more brown materials (fall leaves). Store the dry, brown matter in a tarp-covered pile until you have enough green to mix with it. Newspapers are a cheap source of brown matter.

A 1x4 STABILIZER BOARD, RIGHT, MAY BE NEEDED TO KEEP SIDE WALLS PROPERLY SPACED.

FOR QUICKER COMPOSTING, ADD THIN LAYERS OF SOIL. IT CONTAINS DESIRABLE MICROBES BETWEEN THE LAYERS OF GREEN AND BROWN MATERIALS TO BE COMPOSTED.

THE **4x12**-FT. COMPOSTER ABOVE IS BUILT WITH **2x2**S AND **1x6** BOARDS. IF YOU OPT FOR A LID, RIGHT, USE **2x4** REAR POSTS. USE **1**-IN. CONDUIT FOR THE HINGE, AND ATTACH THE LID USING ELECTRICAL CONDUIT CLAMPS.

Building a Wooden Compost Bin

1 CUT THREE 2x2 PRESSURE-TREATED STAKES **48** IN. LONG. FASTEN **1x6** SIDEBOARDS TO THE STAKES USING GALVANIZED SCREWS, AS SHOWN.

2 CUT OFF EXCESS LENGTH FROM THE TOP OF THE STAKES. NOTE: SPACE THE TWO FRONT STAKES ABOUT 1$\frac{1}{4}$ IN. APART SO THAT FRONT BOARDS WILL SLIDE EASILY.

3 DRIVE STAKES INTO LEVEL GROUND. PROTECT TOPS FROM BEING SPLINTERED WITH SCRAP WOOD. THE BOTTOM BOARDS SHOULD END UP A FEW INCHES FROM THE GROUND.

4 AS YOU DRIVE STAKES TO THE FINAL DEPTH, USE A CARPENTER'S LEVEL TO PLUMB THE STAKES AND LEVEL THE WALL TOPS.

5 FASTEN THE TOPMOST BACK BOARD WITH ONE SCREW AT EACH END; THEN LEVEL THE TWO SIDE PANELS BEFORE INSTALLING THE REMAINING BACK BOARDS.

6 SLIDE BUT DO NOT SCREW THE FRONT BOARDS INTO THE GROOVE BETWEEN THE STAKES. ADD OR REMOVE BOARDS AS NEEDED TO CONTAIN OR REMOVE COMPOST.

Soil Too Sweet or Too Sour

Soil that is too sweet (alkaline) or too sour (acid) can spell big problems for your lawn. It's difficult to know which kind you have, but your region and local annual rainfall can give you clues. Most soils in the eastern third of the United States and Canada, and along the West Coast are naturally acidic. Regions with heavy rainfall tend to have acid soil, too. Moss in a lawn is also a sign of overly acidic soil.

Another indicator of acidity is the age of a lawn. Soil that supports a lawn often becomes more acidic as the seasons pass. Contributing factors include the decomposition of organic matter, the leaching of calcium because of rainfall or irrigation, and the use of acidifying fertilizers and pesticides. Many central and western states have alkaline soils, and low rainfall is the main factor.

Soil acidity is measured in terms of pH, or the amount of hydrogen in the soil, because hydrogen, a common element in most acids, is an indicator of a soil's acidity. Soils with a pH below 7 (neutral) are acidic, or sour. Soils with a pH above 7 are alkaline (non-acidic, or sweet). Most lawn grass varieties grow best with a soil pH between 6 and 7.

The pH scale is logarithmic, so a change of one point indicates a tenfold difference in pH. For example, soil with a pH of 5 is 10 times more acidic than soil with a pH of 6.

The pH level of your soil is important because it determines whether the nutrients in the soil will be available to the grass. For example, phosphorus "locks" with calcium and is unavailable to plants if the soil pH is less than 5.5. Similarly, the soil bacteria that break down nitrogen so that plants can use it thrive when pH is above 4.5. Lawns grown in soils

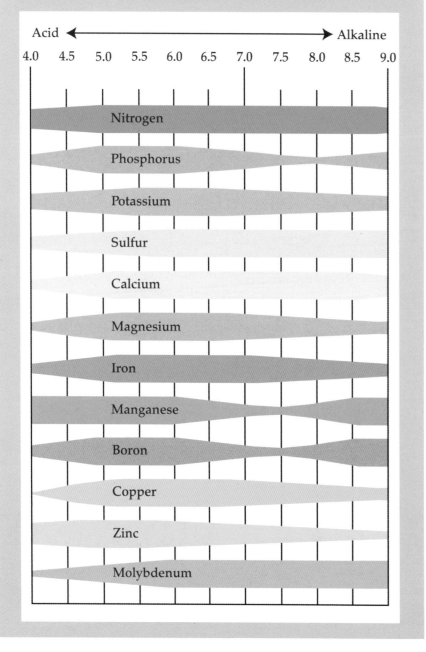

pH and Soil Nutrients

Relative soil acidity greatly affects a plant's ability to absorb nutrients from the soil. For most grasses, the ideal soil pH should be slightly acid, within a range of 5.8 to 6.6. A pH number below 5.5 indicates high soil acidity. A pH number above 8.0 indicates high soil alkalinity. Bar widths approximate the availability of essential nutrients at various pH levels. The narrower the bar width, the less available the nutrient.

Acid ← → Alkaline

| 4.0 | 4.5 | 5.0 | 5.5 | 6.0 | 6.5 | 7.0 | 7.5 | 8.0 | 8.5 | 9.0 |

Nitrogen
Phosphorus
Potassium
Sulfur
Calcium
Magnesium
Iron
Manganese
Boron
Copper
Zinc
Molybdenum

with low pH generally have poor color and are less able to recover from stress.

High pH levels are just as unhealthy for grass as low pH. When soil pH is higher than 8, important nutrients such as phosphorus, iron, and zinc become locked with other elements and are unavailable to the grass.

It is possible to adjust soil pH up or down to a moderate extent. Lime can be added to raise the pH of a soil that is too low. Sulfur can be added to lower the pH of a soil that is too high. But before you set about changing your soil's pH, get a soil test. (See Chapter 3.)

Too Much Shade

Excessive shade can make it difficult to grow dense turf. It inhibits photosynthesis, the process by which plants convert sunlight, inorganic compounds, and carbon dioxide into carbohydrates and energy. Shade-afflicted turf has short roots, thin leaves and stems, and sparse, thin growth. Weakened grass can't tolerate heat, cold, drought, or disease and does not compete well with weeds.

Too much sun, on the other hand, can cause headaches, too. If you're not diligent about watering a sunny lawn, it may burn to a crisp. If too much sun is a problem, consider planting low-growing deciduous ornamental trees on your property, especially to the south or southwest side of lawn areas. Select a species that that will allow some light to reach the lawn.

Sun/Shade Log

Take the time to keep a monthly log through the growing season of how long the sun shines on various parts of your lawn. (To create a sun/shade log, make copies of the chart below). If the lawn receives less than four or five hours of sun a day, your grass is likely to be sparse and may have patches of moss. You may want to consider converting heavily shaded areas to planting beds. Or you can thin low-hanging branches and overseed with a turf seed that's formulated for shade.

Hour	Full Sun	Partial Sun	Full Shade
6:00 a.m.			
6:30 a.m.			
7:00 a.m.			
7:30 a.m.			
8:00 a.m.			
8:30 a.m.			
9:00 a.m.			
9:30 a.m.			
10:00 a.m.			
10:30 a.m.			
11:00 a.m.			
11:30 a.m.			
12:00 noon			
12:30 p.m.			
1:00 p.m.			
1:30 p.m.			
2:00 p.m.			
2:30 p.m.			
3:00 p.m.			
3:30 p.m.			
4:00 p.m.			
4:30 p.m.			
5:00 p.m.			
5:30 p.m.			
6:00 p.m.			
6:30 p.m.			
7:00 p.m.			
7:30 p.m.			
8:00 p.m.			

Thatch Basics

SHORT GRASS ROOTS, ABOVE LEFT, RESULT FROM THATCH BUILDUP THAT EXCEEDS ½ IN. THE THATCH LAYER, LEFT, IS KEPT IN CHECK WITH A ONCE-A-SEASON RAKING WITH A DETHATCHING TOOL, ABOVE. SOME GRASSES, SUCH AS BLUEGRASS, BERMUDAGRASS, AND ZOYSIA, FORM MORE THATCH THAN OTHERS.

Excessive Thatch

Push aside the blades of your lawn grass. If you see a light brown, matted layer of dead and living grass stems, shoots, and roots at the base of the plants, you have thatch. Don't panic. Thatch is a problem only when it is thicker than ½ inch. When it is less than ½ inch, thatch can actually benefit your lawn by absorbing impact from foot traffic and acting like a mulch to insulate your soil from extreme temperatures.

A thick layer of thatch, however, can be harmful. It can prevent water and nutrients from getting to the grass roots, encourage chinch bugs, and foster diseases. When you're restoring a lawn, thatch of any thickness makes it difficult for seed, fertilizer, and other amendments to reach the soil.

If you find thatch in your lawn, study the thatch and determine how much of the root system is in the thatch. If most of the root system is in the thatch, the roots will be less able to take up and store water and elements used for food production. In healthy turf, roots will reach at least 6 to 8 inches deep.

Thatch can be caused by conditions that reduce the number of microbes and earthworms that would otherwise decompose the thatch. These conditions include highly acidic soil, overfertilization, and the use of pesticides. Bluegrass, Bermudagrass, and zoysia are grass species more likely to form thatch than perennial ryegrass or tall fescues. For information on how to remove thatch and maintain your lawn in a way that will prevent its recurrence, see Chapter 3.

This steeply sloped lawn shows pockets of erosion from rain running down the hill before it can be absorbed by the soil. In time, the erosion will worsen unless corrective measures are taken.

Bare Spots, Erosion, and Standing Water

Are areas in your lawn tough to keep covered with turf? Heavy foot or vehicle traffic is usually the culprit. The constant abrasion makes it hard for grass to establish itself, and the compacted soil weakens the grass. Exposure to excessive water flow can also keep grass from thriving. This usually happens at the base of your rain gutter leaders and along the road near storm drains. Standing water that covers the surface for more than four days can also smother and kill the grass.

Wear resulting from foot traffic can often be avoided by installing a path of durable material, such as slate, gravel, brick, or even pressure-treated lumber.

Preventing water erosion is more involved. If the source of the water is a roof via a leader or downspout, a dry well will help drain water away. If the problem is running or standing surface water, you must either improve the grading on your property or provide better drainage in the problem areas. (See "Solve Poor Drainage" in Chapter 9.)

Diseases, Insects, and Weeds

If your examination turns up one or more of this dreaded trio, don't panic and reach for chemical treatments. Most lawns exhibit some weed growth or small areas of disease or insect activity. This is normal. When kept in balance on a healthy lawn by competition from beneficial microorganisms, fungi, and insects, pest populations remain small enough that they aren't considered serious. When a pest does get out of hand, improving your lawn-care practices may be all that's needed to tip the scales back in favor of your turf.

But staying a step ahead of trouble requires you to check your lawn regularly for signs that the problem is either clearing up or worsening. If you suspect you have a problem that improved maintenance alone cannot handle, see Chapters 10, 11, and 12. They will help you determine what ails your lawn and show you ways to improve the situation using the least toxic methods.

Irregular Surface

An uneven lawn can be unattractive to look at, uncomfortable to walk on, and even difficult to mow. Depressions, holes, and ruts can be caused by erosion, car traffic, or industrious rodents—such as moles, voles, and woodchucks—or by removed tree stumps, buried roots, or logs that decay and cause voids under the lawn. Repair such irregularities before restoring or replanting your lawn.

Reducing fertilization, controlling thatch, and raising your cutting blade will often be enough to ward off infestations from grass munchers, such as this chinch bug.

Weeds, such as the annual bluegrass above, are a sign of soil infertility. Addressing the root cause of the problem will help prevent its reoccurrence.

Small areas of grass disease, right, can typically be handled by changing management practices and rarely require starting a new lawn from scratch.

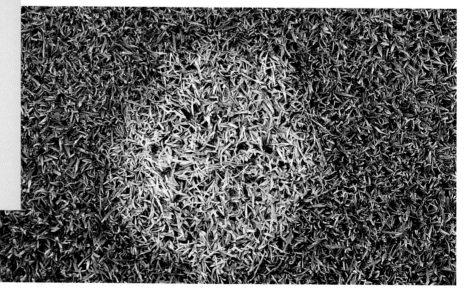

Vehicular traffic, especially while the turf is rain-soaked or frozen, will compact the soil and create an irregular surface.

Fill holes and depressions in your lawn to prevent scalping and to make for smooth mowing. Bumps can cause nuts and bolts to loosen.

Bare paths are the result of heavy foot traffic. Repair of such damage will require a complete lawn overhaul.

SCORE SHEET

Rate the Condition of Your Turf

To get a clear picture of your lawn's health, examine it aboveground and belowground. Don't rely on your memory for this exercise. Walk through your property with this score sheet, making observations firsthand. Place a check next to the statements that best describe what you find. When you're done, add up your total points, and match that total to the Score Guide on the opposite page.

Health of Grass Plants

❑ (3 pts.) Most grass plants in your lawn are strong and have full blades with a deep green color.
❑ (2 pts.) Some grass blades are thin or have a yellow-green cast.
❑ (1 pt.) Most grass blades are thin with yellow or brown spots during the growing season.

Turf Density

❑ (3 pts.) The grass plants form a tight-knit "carpet" with hardly any soil visible; the grass is thick, even where there's foot traffic.
❑ (2 pts.) Turf covers the lawn pretty evenly, yet small areas of soil show; some wear shows in high-traffic areas.
❑ (1 pt.) Areas as large as 3 or 4 inches in diameter show frequently between grass clumps; bare spots are prevalent in lawn areas used for paths or recreation.

Drainage

❑ (3 pts.) Rain is absorbed by your lawn and rarely runs off into storm sewers, ponds, or streams—even after heavy downpours.
❑ (2 pts.) Your lawn has several areas of bare soil resulting from erosion, especially near downspouts; rainwater sometimes seeps into your basement or runs to the street after moderate rainfall.
❑ (1 pt.) In addition to basement or street runoff problems, you have standing water on your lawn after rainstorms.

Weed Presence

❑ (3 pts.) Less than one-fourth of your lawn is infested with weeds.
❑ (2 pts.) Between one-half and one-fourth of your lawn is covered with weeds.
❑ (1 pt.) One-half or more of your lawn is infested with weeds.

Think of your weed-control strategy as two-pronged: to promote healthy grass as well as to reduce weed growth.

Did You Know? *Grass clippings do not increase the thatch layer. They are 75 to 85 percent water and decompose quickly. In fact, 100 pounds of grass clippings can generate and recycle as much as 3 to 4 pounds of nitrogen, ½ to 1 pound of phosphorus, and 2 to 3 pounds of potassium back to the lawn every year.*

Evenness of Surface
❑ (3 pts.) Your lawn feels level when walked upon; it has no holes or ruts.
❑ (2 pts.) There are occasional bumps and depressions.
❑ (1 pt.) There are many holes or ruts.

Root Length
❑ (3 pts.) Grass roots are 6 to 12 inches long.
❑ (2 pts.) Grass roots are 3 to 6 inches long.
❑ (1 pt.) Grass roots tend to be less than 3 inches long.

Soil Texture
❑ (3 pts.) You can easily push a screwdriver or spade deeply into the soil.
❑ (2 pts.) A screwdriver or spade penetrates soil to a depth of 3 or 4 inches before pushing becomes difficult.
❑ (1 pt.) It is difficult to push a screwdriver or spade into the soil.

Earthworm Population
❑ (3 pts.) There are two or more earthworms in a spadeful of lawn soil.
❑ (2 pts.) There is one earthworm per spadeful.
❑ (1 pt.) There are usually no worms in a spadeful of soil.

Thatch
❑ (3 pts.) A ½-inch layer or less of dead shoots, stems, and roots has formed at the base of your grass plants.
❑ (2 pts.) The thatch layer is ½ to 1½ inches thick.
❑ (1 pt.) The thatch layer is more than 1½ inches thick.

Organic Material
❑ (3 pts.) The dark top layer of your soil is more than 5 inches deep.
❑ (2 pts.) The top layer of soil is between 3 and 5 inches deep.
❑ (1 pt.) The top layer of soil is less than 3 inches deep.

Score Guide

26–30 Your turf is in great shape. Proceed to Chapter 7 and review the recommended low-maintenance lawn-care program.

20–25 Better maintenance should renew your lawn. If new lawn-care practices don't improve your lawn's condition, proceed with a lawn restoration, as described in Chapter 3.

15–19 Your lawn is a good candidate for restoration.

10–14 Your turf should probably be removed so that you can improve the soil and replant.

Restoring a Tired Lawn

A restoration allows you to improve your lawn without removing the existing turf. You'll have the best chance of success if your lawn scored more than 15 points on the "Rate the Condition of Your Turf" score sheet in Chapter 2—and if you did not make major changes in design. While restoring your lawn is not nearly as labor intensive as removing all of your turf and starting over, it will still require several weekends of work. In this chapter, each step of a lawn restoration is described, some of which are essential and others optional. In most parts of North America, the best time to begin restoration is late summer or early fall, although adjusting pH and dethatching can be done in the spring to prepare for a fall restoration. You will see some improvement in a restored lawn during the season in which you begin, but you will need two or three growing seasons to see dramatic progress.

Pruning of damaged and unwanted tree limbs can give grass more hours of direct sunlight.

Improve Your Soil

Horticulturists agree that time spent improving what's happening below the surface of a lawn greatly reduces the time needed to maintain what's on top of it. The ideal soil for grass meets five requirements: it (1) is slightly acid, (2) contains an adequate supply of nutrients, (3) allows deep root growth, (4) supports a thriving population of beneficial microbes, and (5) retains adequate moisture. You can achieve these ideal conditions by adding various amendments to your soil. For example, applications of lime or sulfur will modify pH. Fertilizers can supplement the nutrients already in your soil. And organic material can improve soil structure and the soil's ability to retain water and to support microbial activity.

Collecting Soil Samples

1 TAKE SOIL SAMPLES FROM VARIOUS AREAS IN YOUR YARD USING A TROWEL.

2 MIX THE SAMPLES IN A PLASTIC BUCKET.

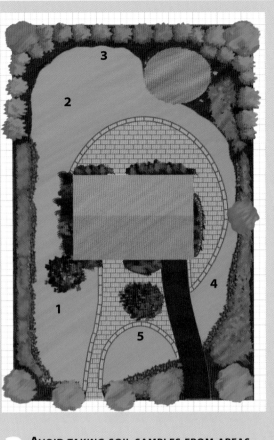

3 AVOID TAKING SOIL SAMPLES FROM AREAS LIKELY TO HAVE DIFFERING MAKEUPS. FOR EXAMPLE, AREA **3** IN THE ILLUSTRATION ABOVE WAS FORMERLY A VEGETABLE GARDEN. IN AREA **4**, THE TOPSOIL WAS IMPORTED FROM ANOTHER PROPERTY.

Getting a Soil Test

To learn which amendments and how much of them to add to your lawn, you need to have your soil tested. The best way to test your soil is to send a sample to a Cooperative Extension Service (usually located at or affiliated with a state university) or commercial soil laboratory. You can check the Yellow Pages under " Laboratories—Testing" for commercial soil-testing labs. Most test results indicate the pH and nutrient content of the soil, and they will tell you what to add to achieve the correct pH and nutrient levels. Some labs will also tell you what type of soil you have and how much organic mate-

rial your soil contains. (For information on using do-it-yourself soil tests, see "Do-It-Yourself Soil Tests" on page 47.)

Kits from soil labs provide instructions for collecting soil samples and a mailing container for returning the soil. Typically, you will be asked to use a clean, rust-free trowel to take samples from up to 10 areas of your lawn. To collect samples, dig several holes in the lawn 6 to 8 inches deep. Take a slice of soil from one side of each hole, save 1 to 2 inches from the middle of the slice, and discard the sides, top, and bottom. You will then be directed to mix the samples in a clear container, allow them to dry at

Sample Test Report

Cornell Nutrient Analysis Laboratories
New York State College of Agriculture and Life Sciences • A Statutory College of the State University
804 Bradfield Hall, Cornell University, Ithaca, NY 14853 • 607/255-4540

LAB INFORMATION

ROUTING	COUNTY	SENT TO COUNTY	REPORT DATE	LAB ID
Grower	WEST	WEST	11/04/88	9000- 6 (K)

ADDRESSES

REPRESENTATIVE	GROWER	COOPERATIVE EXTENSION AGENT
	Ms. Homeowner	ROBERT MARTIN
	123 Main Street	COOPERATIVE EXTENSION
	Anywhere, USA	214 CENTRAL AVE.
		WHITE PLAINS NY 10606

Agents Phone: 914-682-3072

BACKGROUND INFORMATION

IDENTIFICATION	SITE	CROP	TURFGRASS	TREES AND SHRUBS	AMENDMENTS
Bag Number:14979	Environment:MOST SUN	Crop Code:LAW	Species :LAWN MIX	Age/ht/dia:	Manure Typ:
Sample ID :TURF 1K	Drainage :GOOD	Variety :LAW	Cut Height:1 - 2	Location :	Manure,#/A:
Sampled :03/17/88	Texture :LOAMY	Recommend:MAINTENANCE	Clippings :RETURNED	Top Prune :	Compost,in:
Received :07/28/88	Topography :TOP	Month :	Irrigation:SCHED.	Tree Type :	Lime, #/M: 50 04/01/8
			Irr. Rate : 1 in/wk	Growth :	Sulfar #/M:

SOIL TEST RESULTS

			Very Low	Low	Medium	High	Excess
pH		5.8					
PHOSPHORUS	(P #/A)	21					
POTASSIUM	(K #/A)	180					
MAGNESIUM	(Mg #/A)	140					
CALCIUM	(Ca #/A)	1370					

Ex Acidity (ME/100g):	14	Manganese	(Mn #/A):	29	Nitrate		23
Aluminum	(Al #/A):	192	Zinc	(Zn #/A):	3.3	Salts (mmho/cm):	0.190
Iron	(Fe #/A):	20	Organic Matter	(%):	4.1	Salts (K x 1000:1):	19

LIME AND FERTILIZER RECOMMENDATIONS

····· Recommendations per acre ········		··· Recommendations per 1000 sq ft ···		···· Recommendations per 100 sq ft ····		
Lime	(T/A): 5	Lime	45	Lime	(#/100 sq ft):	20.7
Nitrogen	(N #/A): 130	Nitrogen	2.0	Nitrogen	(#/100 sq ft):	0.30
Phosphate (P205 #/A): 0		Phosphate	2.0	Phosphate	(#/100 sq ft):	0
Potash	(K20 #/A): 120	Potash	2.0	Potash	(#/100 sq ft):	0.28

1ST YEAR, LAWN (LAW)
1. MAINTAIN A GOOD SAMPLING PROGRAM AND KEEP A RECORD OF ALL NUTRIENT ANALYSES AND RECOMMENDATIONS.
2. IF AN ANALYSIS RESULT IS NOT REFFERED TO SPECIFICALLY IN THE RECOMMENDATIONS OR COMMENTS THEN LEVELS ARE CONSIDERED NORMAL.
3. NITROGEN SHOULD BE APPLIED AT RATES OF 0.5 TO 1 #/M. HIGHER RATES MAY BE USED WHEN SLOW RELEASE SOURCES ARE USED.
4. THE RECOMMENDED RATES ABOVE ARE AN ANNUAL NUTRIENT REQUIREMENT FOR THIS CROP.
5. IF WATER SOLUBLE SOURCES ARE USED, WATER IN AFTER APPLICATION.
6. LIME RATE IS FOR 100% ENV. TO CALCULATE ACTUAL RATE: RATE TO USE = RECOMMENDED RATE/ENV (OF LIME SOURCE) X 100.
7. APPLY NO MORE THAN 80 #/A (2 #/M) OF POTASH PER APPLICATION.
8. THE MAXIMUM RATE OF LIME RECOMMENDED FOR TOPDRESSING AN ESTABLISHED TURF IS 1 T/A (50 #/M).
9. NITROGEN RECOMMENDATIONS IN THE TABLE ABOVE ARE FOR THE ENTIRE YEAR.

Abbreviation key: lb = pound, # = pound, T = tons, A = acres, M = 1000, N = nitrogen, and SQ FT = square feet.

BACKGROUND IN

CROP

SUN	Crop Code:LAW	Spe
	Variety :LAWN	Cut
	Recommend:MAINTENANCE	Cli
	Month :	Irr
		Irr

SOIL TEST

pH			5.8	Very-L
PHOSPHORUS	(P	#/A)	21	
POTASSIUM	(K	#/A)	180	
MAGNESIUM	(Mg	#/A)	140	
CALCIUM	(Ca	#/A)	1370	

Ex Acidity (ME/100g):	14	Mang
Aluminum	(Al #/A): 192	Zinc
Iron	(Fe #/A): 20	Orga

FERTILIZER RECOMMENDATIO

··· Recommendations per 1000 sq ft ···		···· Rec
Lime	45	Lime
Nitrogen	2.0	Nitroge
Phosphate	2.0	Phospha
Potash	2.0	Potash

LAB TEST REPORTS CAN BE CONFUSING. DO NOT HESITATE TO CALL THE SOURCE FOR HELP. THIS REPORT INCLUDES MAINTENANCE RECOMMENDATIONS, pH AND NUTRIENT READINGS, AND THE AMOUNTS OF FERTILIZER TO APPLY.

room temperature, enclose a small fee, and send it all to the lab. Lab tests from state universities usually cost around $20, including the return postage. Commercial lab tests can cost more than $100, depending on the amount of information you request. The best time to test soil is in the spring, before you have added any compost or other amendments, although you can test soil at any time of the year.

If your yard has lawn areas that range over various types of terrain (for example, near a pond or brook, a rocky ledge, or an area with imported topsoil), you should request a separate sampling kit for each area. Otherwise the lab may recommend doses of fertilizer or soil amendments that are suitable for one area but not for another.

Test results will tell you what you need to add to your soil. There are two ways to add these materials. If you have an acceptable lawn but are looking to improve it, you may spread these materials over the lawn surface. This chapter covers lawn restoration and explains the best way to accomplish this. It also explains how to aerate the turf with a core cultivator after you've applied amendments. Aeration will help mix the amendments with the top layer of soil and will help loosen the top layer of mildly compacted soil. If your lawn is beyond restoration by mere surface treatment and you have opted to till amendments into the topsoil, turn to Chapter 4. There you'll find step-by-step instructions on how to rebuild soil and replant the lawn.

Test Soil Yourself

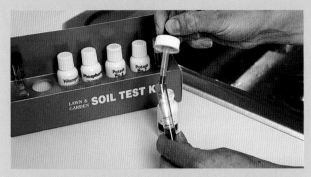

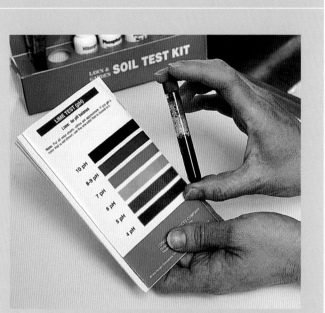

1 TO TEST YOUR SOIL, ADD THE APPROPRIATE SOLU-
TION TO A MEASURED AMOUNT OF THE SOIL SAM-
PLE PER THE MANUFACTURER'S INSTRUCTIONS.

3 MATCH THE COLOR OF THE RESULTING SOLUTION
WITH THE COLOR CHART PROVIDED TO DETERMINE
pH OR NUTRIENT LEVELS. THE CHART HERE SUGGESTS
A pH OF SLIGHTLY MORE THAN 5, INDICATING ACIDIC
SOIL AND THE NEED FOR AN APPLICATION OF LIME.

2 SHAKE THE SOLUTION WELL AND ALLOW THE PAR-
TICLES TO SETTLE.

DO-IT-YOURSELF SOIL TESTS

Smart **TIP**

The costs for multiple lab tests, even at nominal lab fees, will add up quickly. If you need to make more than four or five tests on your property, you will probably want to buy your own soil test kit. Soil test kits range from about $5 for a pH tester capable of doing 10 separate tests to about $10 for a kit that also lets you test basic nutrients (nitrogen, phosphorus, and potash). Kits are available at most garden-supply stores.

These kits are not a substitute for professional soil testing. They do not tell you how much soil amendment to add to achieve desired pH or nutrient levels. The test kits are an inexpensive, quick way to test several areas and will give you a general idea of your soil's deficiencies. Once you have professional soil test results, you may opt to use your own tests to monitor the progress of the soil improvements you make.

To dethatch a lawn in preparation for overseeding, first mow grass to about 1 in. Then, using a thatching rake, use push and pull strokes to lift the thatch. If you have a large lawn, rent a power rake.

Steps to Restoring a Lawn

STEP 1: Remove Thatch and Weeds

When beginning a lawn restoration, the first step is to remove any thatch buildup—even low levels that would otherwise be acceptable. Unless you can expose the soil between the old grass plants, the steps that follow will have poor results. While you're at it, make a note of weed colonies, and remove the worst of them using a grape (grubbing) hoe before proceeding to Step 2.

The best time to dethatch is when your lawn is thriving—not when it's stressed in the heat of summer or cold of winter. To begin, set the height adjustment on your mower to cut the grass to about 1 inch high, essentially half its normal mowing height. Mow the entire lawn. Short grass will make dethatching and surface preparation easier. It will also improve seed germination rates because more seed will make contact with the soil and seedlings will have better exposure to the sun.

The easiest way to remove thatch from a lawn that is more than 3,000 square feet is by using a power rake, or vertical mower (a machine with vertical instead of horizontal cutting blades), which should be available at rental stores. For smaller lawns or lawns with thin layers of thatch (½ to 1 inch), a manual thatching rake will do a satisfactory job.

When using a vertical mower to remove average amounts of thatch and to scarify the soil, set the blades to cut ⅛ to ¼ inch into the soil. Make several test passes on an inconspicuous area of your lawn to judge how much thatch (and turf) will be removed. If too much or too little is removed, raise or lower the blades accordingly. The spacing between blades can be adjusted on some machines, but this is difficult to do and is best done by the rental-store staff. The blade spacing for Bermudagrass and zoysiagrass is 1 to 2 inches, while the spacing for bahiagrass and St. Augustinegrass is 3 inches. Most rental-store owners will know the optimal settings for the grasses grown in your area.

When using a vertical mower to dethatch, make several passes over the lawn in perpendicular directions. It is important to be thorough. Remove the thatch that you pull up after each series of passes, and add it to your compost pile. When you have finished dethatching, remow your lawn to a height of 1 inch. For more information on manual-thatching rakes and vertical mowers, see Chapter 6.

On a lawn with very thick thatch (more than 1½ inches), you may need to partially remove the thatch and allow the lawn to fully recover before the next dethatching session. Removing too much thatch all at once can do more harm than good. The rule of thumb is to remove what you can without tearing up holes of more than a couple of square inches in live turf. This may not be possible on lawns with very thick thatch (more than 2 inches). In that case, your lawn may not be salvageable and may need to be replanted from scratch. (See Chapter 4.)

STEP 2: Fill Depressions and Level Bumps

While you are dethatching your lawn, check for bumps and depressions. These may have been caused by poor grading, uneven settling, or the decomposition of buried tree stumps, logs, or roots. Mark any irregularities with latex spray paint so that you can find them easily when you're ready to level them.

Smart TIP

BEFORE YOU RESTORE

Now is the time to make landscape improvements, such as grading for better drainage, installing sprinkler systems (if necessary), removing old tree stumps, thinning tree boughs, and felling expendable trees to allow more sunlight. It's also the time for installing drain fields, dry wells, paths, and driveways. Once your new or restored lawn is established, you won't want to ruin it by bringing in heavy equipment, such as earth movers, stump grinders, or wood chippers, to make landscape improvements.

Filling a Depression

1 WHEN FILLING A DEPRESSION IN YOUR LAWN, USE A SPADE TO CUT THE TURF AROUND THE AFFECTED AREA ON THREE SIDES. TRY NOT TO DAMAGE THE ROOTS.

2 CAREFULLY ROLL BACK THE TURF. WITH THE TURF ROLLED BACK, FILL THE DEPRESSION WITH A MIXTURE OF SOIL, COMPOST, AND FERTILIZER.

3 ROLL THE TURF BACK INTO PLACE.

4 SIFT SOIL INTO THE SEAMS. TAMP LIGHTLY AND WATER THOROUGHLY.

To level small bumps, raise the sod using a sharp spade, and remove the necessary amount of soil beneath it. Cut out at least a 2 x 2-foot section of sod. If you lift smaller patches of sod, they will likely dry out and die. While the soil base is exposed, mix in some compost and fertilizer. Soak the area using a hose; press the sod back into place; and sprinkle some soil into the seams. Keep the area watered to prevent lawn brown-out.

Slight depressions can be smoothed over by top-dressing—applying a combination of topsoil and compost to the surface topsoil. A wide landscaping rake is the best tool for this job. When handling larger depressions—those more than an inch or two deep and several square feet in area—raise the sod; fill the depression with a mixture of soil, humus, and fertilizer; replace the sod; and press it in place. Be sure to keep repaired areas moist, or the edges will dry out and turn brown.

STEP 3: Adjust Your Soil's pH

Before applying anything, it's best to test your own soil or obtain test results from a professional testing service. If your soil test shows that the soil pH is low, add lime according to the test recommendations. If you did your own pH test and thus have no recommendations to go by, use the table on page 52, "To Raise pH," to determine how much lime to apply. If you're unsure of your test results, be conservative. Too much of an amendment can be as detrimental to your lawn as none at all.

Lime amendments come in various forms, from ground oyster shells to liquids. Agricultural-ground limestone is the preferred type because it is readily available and can be safely, easily, and accurately applied using a drop or rotary spreader.

There are two types of agricultural ground limestone: dolomitic and calcitic. Both contain calcium carbonate, a grass nutrient, and a neutralizer for acidic soil. Dolomitic limestone contains magnesium, another important nutrient, as well as calcium carbonate. Use dolomitic limestone if your soil is deficient in magnesium. Calcitic limestone does not contain magnesium, making it more appropriate if your soil is already high in magnesium. However, adding dolomitic limestone to soil already high in magnesium has not been shown to cause lawn problems.

For faster results, choose a finely ground limestone. Fine grinds begin to correct the soil pH faster than coarse grinds. Coarsely ground limestone acts slowly and is better suited for use once you have raised your pH to a desirable range. You can tell fine lime from coarse if you understand the information on the package. The higher the percentage of ground lime that passes through the finer sieves, the finer the grind. Sieves are graded by number; the higher the number, the smaller the sieve holes. Look for a product stating that 50 percent or more of the ground limestone will pass through a Number 100 sieve.

One more thing to keep in mind when buying lime is its relative purity. Liming materials are rated according to their Calcium Carbonate Equivalent (CCE). A CCE rating of 100 is equal to pure calcium carbonate; less than 100 indicates less neutralizing ability than calcium carbonate. Account for the CCE when figuring how much lime to apply to your lawn. If the CCE of the product you purchase is 80 and your soil test recommendations assume a CCE of 100, you will need to increase the recommended application rate by 20 percent.

Applying Lime

1 TO MINIMIZE DUST AND ENSURE UNIFORM COVERAGE WHEN APPLYING LIME TO ACID SOILS, USE A PELLETIZED LIME. THIS IS A FINELY GROUND LIMESTONE THAT HAS BEEN MIXED WITH A WATER-SOLUBLE BINDER TO FORM PELLETS.

2 IN THIS CASE THE PELLETIZED LIME IS BEING APPLIED USING A DROP SPREADER, BUT IT CAN ALSO BE APPLIED WITH A ROTARY-TYPE SPREADER.

As shown in the table on page 52, the more clay and organic content in your soil, the more lime you will need to correct the pH. Sandy soils require less lime to raise pH. If you need to add more that 40 pounds of lime per 1,000 square feet to correct your pH, do it in two or more applications.

To Raise pH

The recommendations below are given in pounds per 1,000 square feet when using CCE-rated, finely ground limestone. See page 30 to determine your soil type. Do not add lime if your pH is 6.3 or higher.

pH Adjustment	FESCUES		KENTUCKY BLUE/BERMUDA/RYE	
	5.8–6.2 to 6.5	5.3–5.7 to 6.5	4.8–5.2 to 6.5	4.0–4.7 to 6.5
Sands & Sandy Loams	0	25	50	75
Loams & Clays	0	35	75	100
Sands & Sandy Loams	25	50	75	100
Loams & Clays	35	75	100	100

To Lower pH

The recommendations below are given in pounds per 1,000 square feet when using elemental sulfur. See page 30 to determine your soil type.

pH Adjustment	FESCUES	KENTUCKY BLUE	BERMUDA
	7.5 to 6.5	8 to 6.5	8.5 to 6.5
Loam	18	34	57
Sandy Soil	12	28	46
Clay Soil	23	46	69

Don't apply lime with fertilizer mixed in the same spreader. The resulting chemical reaction will release the nitrogen you want for your grass into the air. After spreading lime, water the lawn to wash the particles off the grass leaves and into the soil.

To lower the pH, add sulfur according to your soil test recommendations. Sulfur amendments are also available in the form of compounds, such as ammonium sulfate. These compounds can be used in place of elemental sulfur, but they can burn turf if used in excess. See amendment packaging for details on amounts that can be safely applied to turfgrass.

If you're relying on your own test kit and not a professional test, follow the recommendations in the table above, "To Lower pH." Sulfur acts within one month to lower soil pH. To avoid applying too much, don't try to make your correction in one application. To meet recommended amounts, make several surface applications a few weeks apart and water the grass after each application.

STEP 4: Add Nutrients

When restoring a lawn, apply the fertilizer as recommended by the results of your soil test. Use a slow-release fertilizer, and avoid putting down more fertilizer than you need. Adding too much nitrogen can cause rapid growth and a thinning of plant cell walls, which makes grass more susceptible to disease. The excess fertilizer may also leach and eventually find its way into waterways, polluting them.

If you did not test your soil, apply a slow-release fertilizer with a nitrogen-phosphorus-potassium ratio of 3-1-2. Apply about ½ pound of nitrogen per 1,000 square feet of lawn. (See "Nitrogen Fertilizers," page 117, for more on fertilizer types.) And remember: do not feed a stressed lawn—adding nutrients to

To add nutrients, use a slow-release fertilizer. It will keep applications to a minimum.

a lawn when you don't know what nutrients are required is like going to the pharmacy and taking medicine when you don't know what's wrong with you. It's best to apply fertilizer at least a week prior to spreading seed. Water it into the soil if it doesn't rain before seeding.

STEP 5: Increase Organic Matter and Microbes

The right dose of fertilizer won't help much if your soil doesn't contain an adequate population of microbes; you need billions of these microscopic organisms per handful. Microbes not only digest grass clippings, dead grass roots, and old stems, but they also make their nutrients available to living grass plants.

To have a thriving microbe population, your soil must contain 2 to 5 percent organic material. A top-dressing of compost mixed with topsoil followed by aeration will eventually incorporate some organic matter into the soil without disrupting the lawn.

When top-dressing your lawn, apply about 1 cubic yard, which is 100 pounds of a 40–60 mix of topsoil and compost, per 1,000 square feet. Topsoil is available from most nurseries and landscape centers.

Building Fertility

1 YOU CAN TOP-DRESS WITH COMPOST TO GIVE YOUR LAWN A BOOST. MIX THE COMPOST AND TOPSOIL TOGETHER IN A WHEELBARROW, AND DUMP PILES AT REGULAR INTERVALS.

2 SPREAD THE COMPOST-SOIL EVENLY USING A WIDE RAKE, AND WORK IT DOWN TO THE ROOTS OF THE GRASS.

Be sure that it has a dark, rich, brown color and that it has not been diluted with lighter-colored subsoils. Compost can be obtained from several sources. Many towns make compost available to residents at little or no cost. They make compost from the leaves, grass, and brush that residents haul to the dump. The compost should be screened to ¼- or ⅜-inch particles, and it should be free of inorganic materials. Its moisture content should be 30 to 50 percent. Any drier, and the compost releases a lot of dust as it's being worked; any wetter, and the

EASIER AERATION

Smart TIP

Thoroughly water (about 1 inch) your lawn one or two days prior to aerating. This will help soften the soil and allow for better penetration by the aerator. If aerating after prolonged rainfall, it's important to wait until the soil has dried somewhat so that soil cores do not stick in the aerator's hollow tines.

material tends to clump and not mix well with soil. Compost is also available from nurseries and landscape centers. Better yet, make your own. (For more on compost, see page 33.)

STEP 6: Aerate Compacted Lawns

Aeration, also called *core cultivation* or *aerifying*, is an important part of any lawn restoration program. It allows grass roots to deeply penetrate the soil, helps fertilizer and organic matter get to the roots, allows oxygen to reach the roots, and makes it easier for water to soak into the soil. Simply aerate once in the fall. Avoid aerating during dry summer months because you may damage an already stressed lawn. Also avoid periods when weed seeds are prevalent, as that could cause weed infestation.

There are several types of aerating tools. Manual aerators allow you to do small areas a little at a time and to aerate corners and other tight areas difficult to reach with large equipment. You supply the power for these tools by pushing the hollow cylinders or corers into the turf—just as you would push in a spade. The tool cuts a plug, or core, that is extracted and deposited on the lawn the next time you push it into the turf. Small power aerators work similarly and are available at rental stores. Some machines use a rotating, tiller-like action that pushes the corers into the soil and extracts small plugs as the machines pull you forward. These lawn mower-size machines will fit into a full-size station wagon, minivan, or pickup truck, and they require two people to transport them.

Avoid aerators that only poke holes in the lawn without removing plugs because they are of less value to your lawn. The largest aerators require a truck and several helpers to transport them, but they do a better job. With these machines, the corers are vertically plunged into the turf to extract a sizable plug. You may opt to have a pro tackle this job.

Aerators penetrate your lawn best when the soil is moist. So unless it rains, water your lawn a day before aerating. When aerating, make several passes in several directions over every square foot of lawn. Next, break up all the plugs extracted by the aerator using the back of a rake or by dragging a metal-mesh doormat or section of chain-link fence over the plugs to spread the soil. You can also mix the soil from the plugs with the topdressing you added in Step 5. Then water thoroughly.

• •

Did You Know? *Contrary to popular belief, wearing golf spikes while working in the yard is not a great way to aerate your lawn. The spikes on golf shoes are less than ½ inch, which isn't nearly long enough to penetrate the soil and reach the roots. Manual aerators, however, are available.*

How to Aerate Soil

Above THIS AERATOR OPERATES BEST WHEN TILTED FORWARD SO THAT ALL OF ITS WEIGHT IS AVAILABLE TO PUSH THE CORERS INTO THE SOIL.

Left THE CORERS RESEMBLE A NARROW SCOOP. THEY DEPOSIT THE CORES ON THE LAWN SURFACE, WHERE THEY WILL BREAK DOWN WITH TIME.

THE CORES WERE EXTRACTED BY THE ROTARY AERATOR SHOWN.

A MANUAL AERATOR DOES A GOOD JOB BUT TAKES A LOT LONGER.

Seed types vary significantly in size. Check the table on the opposite page, as well as your seed producer, for recommendations about application rates for both new and over-seeded lawns.

STEP 7: Prepare the Surface and Overseed It

In the North, the best time to overseed is in late summer and early fall, although you may also try this technique in early spring. Starting in the fall gives the young grass plants a better chance to germinate, establish strong roots, and store food needed for a head start in the spring. In the South, overseed in spring or early summer.

Before you begin, choose the seed that's best for you based on the information in Chapter 5, "Choosing the Right Grass," beginning on page 74. Be sure to select one of the varieties bred to withstand the stresses your lawn faces, and then use the table "How Much Seed to Use When Overseeding" on the opposite page to help you estimate how much seed to buy.

You have several tool options for spreading seed evenly and at the recommended rates. They include your own hands, hand-held and walk-behind spreaders, and slit-seeders, which are power machines that cut shallow slits in the soil and sow seed at the same time. Slit-seeders, available at many rental stores, are the preferred tool, especially if you were not able to remove all thatch prior to overseeding. (See Chapter 6 for more details on these tools.)

If you will be spreading seed by hand or with a spreader, first use a thatching rake to roughen the exposed soil to a depth of ½ inch. Set the spreader to deliver the seed that's recommended by the seed producer for seeding a new lawn, or see the "How Much Seed to Use When Overseeding" table. If you were not able to remove all thatch, sow a little extra seed. Similarly, the higher the percentage of weeds in your lawn, the more seed you should sow.

For sowing grass seed, the recommended approach is to apply seed to the edges of the area you are sowing first. Then divide your seed, and apply half while walking in one direction and the other half while walking in a perpendicular direction. Spread extra seed on bare areas, and lightly cover the seed with a mixture of compost and top-

soil. Then spread more seed on top. Top-dress the seed with a thin layer (¼ to ½ inch) peat moss or shredded straw. Evenly spread the seed about 100 pounds per 1,000 square feet. Watering at this time is critical to prevent the seed from drying out and also to prevent birds and other critters from feasting on it. After applying the top layer of peat or straw, water it well so that the seeds will begin to germinate quickly. Finally, follow up by rolling all seeded areas with a water-weighted roller that is one-third full to press the seed into the soil. These steps will help prevent the seed from drying out rapidly and will thereby improve germination rates.

If you have a lawn with grass that spreads by stolons (aboveground runners), such as Bermudagrass, St. Augustinegrass, zoysiagrass, or buffalograss, you may introduce new grass plants by inserting plugs rather than seed. (See "If you're using plugs," page 72.)

How Much Seed to Use When Overseeding	
Seed Type	Pounds per 1,000 square feet
Bluegrass	1 to 2*
Tall Fescue	4*
Perennial Ryegrass	4*
Fine Fescue	2*

*Note: some experts recommend exceeding these amounts.

Did You Know? *A Cooperative Extension Service is a program between states, counties, and the federal government whose mission is to provide the public with information and education on a variety of topics, including lawn care. Look under the county government section in the blue pages of your phone book to find the nearest office.*

A top layer of straw on an overseeded lawn ensures good germination rates. Do not use hay with seeds, and avoid putting down a heavy straw layer that would inhibit grass growth.

Give Seedlings a Fighting Chance

Below UNTIL GRASS IS ESTABLISHED, WATER AT LEAST TWICE A DAY. DEEP WATERING IS UNNECESSARY. WATER SO THAT THE SOIL IS MOISTENED FOR AN INCH OR SO BELOW THE SURFACE BUT NOT SO PUDDLES OR STREAMLETS FORM. RESUME NORMAL WATERING PATTERNS WHEN GRASS HEIGHT REACHES 2 IN. ONCE AGAIN, DO NOT OVERWATER.

Above UPON EMERGING FROM THE SEED, A FRAGILE YOUNG GRASS PLANT CAN EASILY DRY OUT FROM EXPOSURE TO WIND AND SUN. IT CAN ALSO BE WASHED AWAY IN A DOWNPOUR OR BECAUSE OF OVERWATERING.

STEP 8: Take Care of Young Plants

Your work to this point will have been in vain if you don't care for the young grass plants as the seeds germinate and begin to grow. The most critical need is to apply water at least twice a day, assuming no rain. If the soil is allowed to dry out, the seedlings won't germinate or will soon wither and die. To maximize the germination rate, soak your lawn on the same day you sow the seeds. On the next day, assuming no rain, lightly sprinkle or mist the lawn for about five minutes morning and afternoon. Be sure you have moistened the soil to a depth of 1 inch. Keep the overseeded lawn moist until the young grass plants are 2 inches tall by repeating a light watering every day after periods without rain.

This will take four to six weeks. When the grass is 2 inches tall, resume normal watering patterns. (For tips on setting up a convenient in-ground irrigation system, see Chapter 8, "Lawn Irrigation Systems," beginning on page 120.)

Begin mowing again once the grass reaches 3 to 4 inches but before it is long enough to fall over. Make sure your mower blade is sharp; a dull one may tear up young grass plants. Otherwise, stay off the seeded areas, except to fertilize once more. If needed, apply a second dose of ½ pound of nitrogen per 1,000 square feet six weeks after germination. However, don't add more fertilizer if the grass will soon be dormant because it will do no good at this time.

If you're planning to restore a large lawn, consider installing an in-ground sprinkler system first to ensure success.

Planting a New Lawn

If your lawn suffers from acute soil compaction, rampant weed problems, heavy thatch, or nutrient and organic matter deficiencies, you may want to remove your existing turf and re-plant your lawn. If you're not sure, use the "Rate the Condition of Your Turf" score sheet on page 42. If your lawn scores less than 15 points, or if you've made major design changes, you'll probably need to start over. There are several ways to plant a new lawn: by applying seed, planting either sprigs or plugs, or laying sod. Seeds are applied as discussed in the previous chapter or with a process called hydroseeding, which is spraying seeds in place with a mixture of mulch, water, and nutrients. It's a quick and easy way to get a new lawn fast. Sprigs are typically planted by machine over large lawns. They consist of cut-up lengths of underground or aboveground runners. Plugs are round or square pieces of sod that measure about 2 inches across.

Press seed into a pre-pared soil to lessen the chance of it becoming dislodged by wind or rain.

Comparing Methods

Seeding, a job that even beginners can tackle, is the least expensive planting option. It requires less work than the other planting methods but longer-term care. In most regions, except the South, the best time to seed cool-season grasses is in late summer or early fall, when upper soil mean temperatures are 68° to 86°F. This will allow your new turf to establish roots before the dormant winter period begins, while plant growth is vigorous and competition from weeds is low. Grass plants started in the fall will have a strong start in the spring and a root system sturdy enough to survive the following summer's hot, dry weather. In the South, spring and summer seeding are recommended for warm-season

Planting Methods

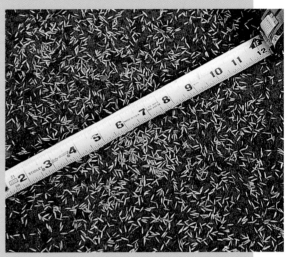

Plugs ARE PLANTED IN HOLES THAT ARE EVENLY SPACED THROUGH-OUT THE LAWN. AFTER SEVERAL MONTHS, THE GRASS PLANTS FROM THE PLUGS SPREAD AND FILL THE GAPS.

Seed IS THE MOST POPULAR WAY TO GET A NEW LAWN. ENSURING ADEQUATE SEED COV-ERAGE AND WATERING ARE KEY TO SUCCESS.

Sprigs CAN BE BROADCAST AND THEN PRESSED INTO THE SOIL OR PLANTED IN SHALLOW FUR-ROWS.

Sod COMES IN CARPET-LIKE SHEETS THAT ARE ABOUT $^3/_4$ IN. THICK, **18** IN. WIDE, AND **6** FT. LONG. IT IS LAID IN A STAG-GERED "BRICK" PATTERN, PERPENDICULAR WITH THE SLOPE.

grasses. The temperature of the upper soil should be 68° to 95°F. Check with your Cooperative Extension Service for the recommended lawn planting times in your area.

Sprigging and plugging are methods typically re-served for warm-season grasses for which seed is not readily available, such as improved strains of Bermudagrass and St. Augustinegrass. Sprigging is best done during the height of the growing season, in spring and summer. Avoid planting when most weeds germinate (spring in the North and fall in the South). It's feasible to plant small areas by either sprigs or plugs. Plugging is generally a more reliable way to generate a new lawn than sprigging, but sprigging is easier to do, and once rooted, sprigs will knit together faster to form turf. In general, sprigs take less time to grow turf than plugs do. Depending on the spacing and type of grass used, it takes several months to grow turf from sprigs and six months or more from plugs.

Spread plastic over areas to be replanted to let heat kill off old turf. Seal the edges with boards or soil.

feasible for homeowners who do not have in-ground sprinkler systems. You will need to take the following steps no matter which method you choose.

STEP 1: Remove Old Turf

The first step is to kill and remove poor-quality turf. There are several ways to do this. For areas where you don't mind a little temporary unsightliness, solarization and heavy mulching are two methods to consider. Solarization bakes grass, weeds, and weed seeds to death under a layer of clear plastic, provided it's securely anchored over the area you want to clear. Cut the old lawn as close to grade as possible before you begin. You'll need two months to achieve the desired effect, provided you install the plastic when the weather is warm. Don't attempt solarization in shady areas or if your summer nights are cool. Smothering ragged turf with heavy mulches, such as old carpeting, 6 inches of wood chips, or several layers of newspaper or large pieces of corrugated cardboard covered by 3 inches of wood chips, will have the same effect.

You may choose to use an herbicide to kill unwanted grass and weeds to the roots. Select an herbicide that degrades quickly (does not last long in the environment), such as glyphosate (Roundup). Mix according to the manufacturer's directions, and completely cover all grass plants and weeds with the solution. Work on a sunny, windless day when the temperature is above 60°F, and take care not to over spray on garden plants. Glyphosate is a potent, non-selective herbicide that will kill or severely injure all foliage it touches. Wear clothing that covers your skin completely, as well as eye protection, when applying this or any other herbicide. Afterward, take a shower and wash your clothing immediately, separately from your regular laundry.

Sod requires more skill to plant, but it's okay to try your luck with small lawns or lawn sections. Sod offers several advantages over seed, plugs, or sprigs. It looks good immediately, and sodded lawns can be used much sooner than lawns planted by the other methods.

Sod is better than seed for planting on sloping terrain, where seed would be washed to low areas after the first hard rain. In addition, sod is less susceptible to erosion while it is becoming established and makes it harder for weeds to compete. Pieces should be laid perpendicular to a slope in a staggered pattern, as you would lay bricks.

Sodding is best done in the fall or spring in the North and in the spring in the South. Plant the sod during cool, humid weather because planting it in warm, dry weather will subject it to burnout. Do not plant sod later than one month before the first fall frost, because you want to give the grass time to establish roots before cold weather sets in.

Steps to Planting a Lawn

Planting a new lawn is a big job. You may want to tackle this in sections. Begin by redoing the worst or most visible lawn areas; then make plans to tackle other areas the following year. This keeps the job manageable and makes the critical step of watering

■ *Removing Old Turf*

1 REMOVE OLD LAWN AFTER A HEAVY RAIN OR DEEP WATER-ING. FIRST MAKE 2-IN.-DEEP CUTS IN THE TURF EVERY 2 FT. USING EITHER A MANUAL OR POWER EDGER, ABOVE.

2 USE A GRAPE (GRUBBING) HOE TO RE-MOVE SMALL SECTIONS OF LAWN. THIS JOB IS EASIER WITH A HELPER.

3 THE IDEA IS TO SLICE THE TURF JUST BELOW THE GRADE. LET THE WEIGHT OF THE TOOL DO THE WORK OF CHIPPING AWAY AT THE GRASS.

4 RENT A POWER SOD CUTTER IF YOU ARE TACKLING A BIG AREA.

You may find that it takes two applications of glyphosate to get the job done. If the turf has not completely died after four weeks, reapply the herbicide, and wait one week after the last application before tilling the dead turf into your soil. Take care to follow the manufacturer's safety precautions.

Mechanical (manual or power) removal of undesirable turf is the fastest way to get the job done without needing to worry about kids or pets contacting herbicides or tracking them into your house. For small lawns, a grape (grubbing) hoe is a terrific tool for removing turf. Anyone with a strong back and a helper to cart away the old turf pieces can remove up to 300 square feet in an hour. For large lawns, consider renting a sod cutter. It slices under the grass, enabling you to pull up strips of old turf. Make the job easier by cutting sod while the lawn soil is moist. Follow up with tilling to alleviate compaction and to prepare the soil for the amendments you'll mix in later. If you have the time, use the solarization technique described on the previous page to kill any weed seeds that remain in the soil.

Puddle Test

1 FOR MAKING MINOR GRADE ADJUSTMENTS, A LAND-SCAPE RAKE IS THE TOOL OF CHOICE.

2 WATER THE AREA. LATER, FILL WHERE PUDDLES FORMED USING SOIL FROM HIGH SPOTS.

STEP 2: Fix Grade Problems

Before adding amendments to the soil, fix any existing grade problems. Although grading often requires help from a landscaping contractor with heavy equipment, minor problems can be fixed by the ambitious do-it-yourselfer. Small versions of earth-moving equipment, such as the Toro Dingo, are often available for sale or for rent.

The first rule of grading is that the ground should slope away from your house in all directions so that it drops at least 2 or 3 inches every 10 feet. The finished grade should also end up matching the level of existing fixtures, such as walkways and patios, as well as areas of established lawn.

This takes some figuring. If you will be replanting with seed and adding 1 inch of amendments, grade so that the level is 1 inch lower than your fixtures. If you will be replanting with sod and adding an inch of amendments, the grade should be about 2 inches lower than your fixtures. Your goal is to have the finished grade—after the sod has been planted and amendments added—even with the level of your fixtures.

The proper way to regrade is first to remove the topsoil from the problem area. Make adjustments to the subsoil by scraping away high areas and filling in low areas. Then spread 2 inches of the reserved topsoil over the subsoil, and till it into the first 2 inches of subsoil. This will help prevent drainage problems between the two layers of soil. Lastly, spread the rest of your topsoil, which should make up at least another 4 inches. If you need to add topsoil, buy a loam that's free of debris, such as roots and stones. It should also be free of weed seeds and pesticides. A landscaping rake is the best tool for working topsoil to the proper grade if you're doing it yourself.

The maximum slope in a lawn should be 12 inches for every 4 feet. If the drop is greater than 12 inches, you should plan to build a low retaining wall or cover the slope with a hardy ground cover or ornamental grass.

STEP 3: Amend the Soil

Now is your chance to add amendments such as fertilizer, organic matter, and lime or sulfur. The opportunity probably won't come again, so don't skimp. The right way to proceed is to add recommended amendments according to the results of your soil test. To have your soil tested, send samples to the local Cooperative Extension Service or a commercial soil-testing lab. The typical recommendations for every 1,000 square feet of new lawn include about 2 pounds of actual (elemental) phosphorus and potassium, 50 to 100 pounds of lime (in areas with acid soil), and 3 to 6 cubic yards of organic matter (such as compost or peat moss). Recommendations will vary depending on your soil's nutrient, organic matter, pH levels, and your particular soil type.

Ensure an even application of amendments by dividing the recommended amounts in half and applying half while walking in one direction and the other half while walking in a perpendicular direction. Once you have applied the amendments, till them into the top 6 inches of soil.

If an overabundance of weeds was one of your reasons for redoing this section of lawn, allow the many weed seeds in the turned soil to sprout. If you rake through or till under the weed seedlings, you can eliminate most annual weeds.

STEP 4: Rake Smooth and Firm

Rake the area to be replanted until it's smooth. Remove any stones and vegetative matter brought to the surface during tilling. Once you're satisfied, water the ground, and check it for puddles. When the soil is dry enough to be worked, move soil from high spots to fill the depressions.

Whether you're planting seed, sprigs, plugs, or sod, it's helpful to roll the prepared soil to provide a firmer base on which to work and to foster adequate soil structure. For example, seed planted in soil that is too loose generally ends up being planted too deeply. The tiny plants may die before they reach the surface. Fill a lawn roller about one-third full of water for this job, and roll the soil until your footprints are no deeper than ½ inch. Complete planting preparations by watering the area thoroughly two days before planting. Check to be sure the soil is moistened to a depth of 5 or 6 inches.

Make Amendments

3 USE A GARDEN RAKE TO REMOVE STONES AND DEBRIS, SUCH AS WEEDS AND LEAVES.

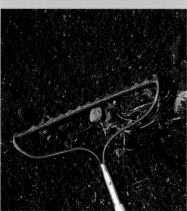

1 ONCE THE GRADE IS SET, EVENLY SPREAD AMENDMENTS, SUCH AS COMPOSTED MANURE, USING A GARDEN RAKE.

2 USE A TILLER TO WORK AMENDMENTS, INCLUDING FERTILIZER AND ORGANIC MATTER, INTO THE SOIL.

4 LEVEL USING A LANDSCAPE RAKE; THEN YOU'RE READY TO SEED OR SOD YOUR LAWN.

1. HAVE SOD DELIVERED TO A SHADY SPOT NEAR YOUR PLANTING SITE.
2. LIGHTLY WATER THE SOIL, AND AVOID WALKING ON IT.
3. START LAYING SOD AT YOUR OUTER LAWN PERIMETER, USING WHOLE SOD WIDTHS.
4. TRY TO WORK IN THE OPPOSITE DIRECTION OF YARD SLOPE.
5. LAY THE NEXT ROW AGAINST THE FIRST, STAGGERING THE JOINTS AND FITTING EACH EDGE SNUGLY.
6. USE CUTOFFS LONGER THAN 2 FT. TO BEGIN NEW ROWS.
7. USE SHORT LENGTHS OF SOD IN ROW INTERIORS.
8. WATER INSTALLED SOD WITHIN 20 MINUTES.
9. KNEEL TO THE SODDED SIDE OF EACH ROW; AVOID DAMAGE TO SOD BY USING A SHEET OF PLYWOOD.
10. TRIM BORDERS AFTER LAYING PIECES USING A SHARP KNIFE OR MANUAL EDGER.

STEP 5: Plant Your New Lawn

If you're using sod

Begin by applying a starter fertilizer high in phosphorus, such as 2:1:1 or 1:1:1 ratio. (See page 117.) Then lightly water the area where you will be installing the sod. Be prepared to begin work when your order is delivered. Sod can go bad quickly, especially if it begins to heat up or dry out. Have the pallets delivered to a shady spot. If you can't start right away, unroll the sod and keep it moist.

Lay sod over one section of lawn at a time. Begin by laying full strips along the outside edge (such as the sidewalk) of the area you plan to sod. Starting with a straight row will reduce the amount of cutting and fitting you'll do later. Next, work toward the opposite edge of lawn, usually the edge by your house. Use a sharp-bladed knife or sod-cutting tool to cut as required. Make your last row a full-width strip, if possible. With contoured borders, overlap the border with sod, and trim away the excess later.

■ *Getting Started*

1 IMMEDIATELY UPON DELIVERY, CHECK SOD FOR DAMAGE, SUCH AS TEARS, A YELLOW-GREEN OR BLUISH COLOR, WEEDS, DISEASE, AND INSECTS. REJECT BAD SOD.

2 PREPARE SOIL FOR SOD BY ROLLING USING A ROLLER THAT IS ONE-THIRD FULL.

3 MOST ROLLERS ARE FILLED AT A HOLE IN THE SIDE OF THE DRUM THAT'S PLUGGED WITH A RUBBER STOPPER.

4 THE ROLLED SOIL SHOULD BE COMPACTED ENOUGH SO THAT FOOTPRINTS ARE NO DEEPER THAN $1/2$ IN.

5 LIGHTLY WATER THE AREA TO BE SODDED, WALKING ON IT AS LITTLE AS POSSIBLE.

6 USE A SHARP KNIFE TO CUT SOD. SOME PROS MAKE A SOD CUTTER BY SHARPENING THE EDGE OF A TROWEL.

Laying Sod

1 Use a sharpened trowel to make it easy to cut sod to fit at butt joints or when cutting against a straightedge.

2 You may also use the trowel to level any minor irregularities in the soil while laying the sod.

5 When fitting sod at odd angles, lay one piece over the other and cut through both at once. Lift the top piece, and remove the waste below.

6 When you have laid sod to the opposite side of the area you're working in, cut the next-to-last piece to fit. Roll out the sod for a test fit first.

9 Where needed, use a sharp edger to trim bed edges.

10 Use a roller to eliminate air pockets that may remain under the newly laid sod.

3 AS YOU LAY THE SOD, KEEP ALL JOINTS AS SNUG AS POSSIBLE, BUT AVOID OVERLAPPING THE SOD. DO NOT STRETCH SOD STRIPS TO FILL GAPS.

4 AFTER YOU HAVE INSTALLED SEVERAL PIECES OF SOD, SPRAY WITH WATER UNTIL THE SOD IS COMPLETELY SOAKED. THIS REQUIRES ABOUT **1** IN. OF WATER.

7 USING A LONG BOARD AS A STRAIGHTEDGE, MAKE YOUR CUT. DISCARD THE PIECE OF WASTE SOD THAT REMAINS.

8 IT'S IMPORTANT TO HAVE FULL STRIPS AT THE PERIMETER. THESE ARE THE STRIPS MOST LIKELY TO DRY OUT AND WILL DO SO MORE QUICKLY IF NARROW OR SHORT.

11 IF ROLLING EXPOSES JOINTS BETWEEN THE SOD STRIPS, FILL THEM WITH FINE SOIL.

12 USE A RAKE TO WORK SOIL INTO SMALL CRACKS.

■ *Cutting Curves*

1 ALONG PATHS, DRIVEWAYS, AND PATIOS, LET SOD STRIPS OVERLAP THE EDGE.

2 THEN TRIM THE EXCESS SOD AS CLOSE TO THE BOARDER AS POSSIBLE.

Again, try to install all the sod the day it's delivered. If you have sod left over, unroll it in a shady spot, water it lightly, and use it the next day. If you do sod your lawn in sections, you will need to lay sod against part of the existing lawn. You may find it helpful to use twine and stakes to mark the dividing line. Use the twine as a guide to cut a straight line in the existing turf using a manual or power edger. Lay sod to this edge, and make a tight, unobtrusive seam. If you're installing sod on a slope, start laying the sod at the lowest point. Stake each piece in three places to prevent slippage. Stakes should be equally spaced and set in from the sod strip's edges by at least 6 to 8 inches.

After installing the sod, firm it by rolling with a roller that is one-third full. If the roller is too heavy, it could cause the sod to slip. In hot weather, lightly watering the sod prior to rolling will also help prevent slippage. Follow rolling immediately with a thorough soaking—to a soil depth of 6 to 8 inches—and restrict traffic for several weeks.

To anchor sod on a steep slope and keep it from slipping, drive thin wood stakes through it.

If you're using seed

Apply a starter fertilizer (one with a nutrient ratio of 1:1:1 or 1:2:1) to the prepared surface, but do not till it in. Spread the best seed you can afford at the rate recommended by the seed packager. (Rates are usually given in pounds per 1,000 square feet.)

In the absence of specific recommendations from the seed packager, the rule of thumb for seed coverage is 15 to 20 seeds per square inch. Make trial passes with your spreader, and adjust it until you achieve seven or eight seeds per square inch. Spread seed in two passes, first in one direction and then in a perpendicular direction, to ensure even coverage of about 15 seeds per square inch. Bulk up seed using vermiculite or sand if your spreader delivers too much seed even when set on the lowest setting. Follow up with a light raking to work the seed into the top ⅛ inch of soil; a light rolling with an empty roller will ensure good seed contact with the soil.

Seeding sloped areas is difficult because the seed tends to run to low points when it rains. One solution is to contract with a landscaper who has hydroseeding equipment. Hydroseeding involves spraying a suspension of fertilizer, mulch, and water onto the prepared surface. Apply frequent light waterings to hydroseeded surfaces to keep them from drying out.

The Amount of Seed to Use for New Lawns

Seed Type	Pounds per 1,000 square feet
Kentucky Bluegrass	2 to 3
Tall Fescue	5 to 7
Perennial Ryegrass	4 to 6
Fine Fescue	4

Note: setter spreadings vary with type and model of spreader. Consult your owner's manual for exact settings. Apply 50 percent more seed if you are attempting to sow a new lawn in the spring.

▪ Seed Coverage

THE RULE OF THUMB FOR SEED COVERAGE IS **15 TO 20** SEEDS PER SQ. IN.—LESS WHEN CONDITIONS ARE FAVORABLE, MORE WHEN THEY ARE NOT.

TO IMPROVE GERMINATION RATE, RAKE THE SEEDED SURFACE LIGHTLY TO MIX SEED WITH THE TOP ⅛ IN. OF SOIL, AND THEN ROLL USING AN EMPTY ROLLER.

Sprigs and Plugs

Plant sprigs SO THAT THE TOP QUARTER OF EACH PLANT IS EXPOSED. SPACE SPRIGS **6** TO **12** IN. APART, DE-PENDING ON THE GRASS TYPE.

Plant plugs 6 TO **12** IN. APART, AGAIN DEPENDING ON GRASS TYPE AND GROWER RECOMMENDATIONS.

If you're using sprigs

There are two ways to plant sprigs by hand. You can broadcast, or stolonize, sprigs over prepared soil at a rate of 5 to 10 bushels per 1,000 square feet, cover with ¼ to ½ inch of soil, and then press the sprigs into the soil by rolling. Or you can plant the sprigs in shallow furrows, 1 to 2 inches deep and 6 to 12 inches apart, depending on the grass variety and the sprig producer's spacing recommendations. Plant sprigs in furrows, end-to-end at 4- to 6-inch intervals, and cover with soil. Be sure a portion of each sprig remains exposed to light—ideally one-quarter of its length—and then lightly roll or tamp the planted area to press the sprigs into the soil.

If you're using plugs

Plant plugs every 6 to 12 inches in furrows 6 to 12 inches apart, or plant them in holes spaced 6 to 12 inches apart in each direction. If you're digging individual holes, using a bulb planter will make the job go quicker. Plant slower-spreading grasses, such as zoysiagrass, 6 inches apart because of their slow growth rates. Grasses that spread more quickly,

such as St. Augustinegrass or Bermudagrass, may be planted farther apart. You can purchase plugs or make your own from unwanted areas of turf. Use a golf-green cup cutter to cut circular plugs, or use a sharp knife, such as a machete, to cut 2-inch-square plugs.

STEP 6: Caring for Your New Lawn

Once your new lawn is planted, take precautions to prevent it from being damaged. Minimize play and foot traffic on newly planted lawns, including sodded lawns, for at least three weeks. Plan for watering needs before you plant your lawn, not afterward. Insufficient water is the leading cause of new-lawn failure, and overwatering is not far behind.

For newly seeded lawns, set sprinklers to mist the surface four times a day, beginning at 7 A.M. and finishing at 6 P.M. The seedbed should be kept moist, but not saturated, to a depth of 1 to 2 inches. As seedlings grow to a height of 2 inches, reduce the frequency but increase the depth of waterings.

For plugs, sprigs, or sod, water at least twice a day, including once during midday. Keep the soil moist

PROTECT WITH STRAW

Smart TIP

If the weather is dry or warm, spread a layer of straw mulch over seeded areas. Choose a clean mulching straw that's free of seed, such as wheat straw. Evenly spread about 50 to 80 pounds (one or two bales) per 1,000 square feet. In windy areas, stretch string over the mulch every few feet to keep it from blowing away. Avoid putting down a heavy layer that would inhibit grass growth. Burlap and agricultural fleece (a textile mulch that admits water and sunlight) are other mulches that will protect the seed from drying sun and wind. They are particularly helpful in preventing erosion and seed runoff when staked over seeded slopes. You may remove mulches approximately three weeks after germination.

Spread straw mulch over a new lawn to slow evaporation, provide some shade, and disperse raindrops that might otherwise dislodge young seedlings.

to a depth of 1 to 2 inches. Check, however, to be sure that the soil does not stay saturated for long periods; otherwise the plants may not root. Reduce watering frequency to every second or third day once a sodded, sprigged, or plugged lawn has begun new root growth (about two weeks). After four weeks, a sodded lawn can survive longer periods without water.

Begin mowing newly seeded, sprigged, and plugged lawns after the grass has grown to a height of 3 or 4 inches but before it falls over in a slight breeze. Set the throttle of your mower on low to help prevent seedlings from being uprooted. For your first mowing, remove just enough (½ to ¾ inch) to give your lawn an even appearance. Next time,

cut to the maximum height recommended for your type of grass, but do not remove more than 30 percent of the blade in any single mowing.

Do not mow a sodded lawn for at least 10 days after installation and not until the grass has begun to grow vigorously. Once again, if you use a rotary mower, set the throttle low to avoid lifting and chopping up pieces of sod. Once sprigs and plugs are established, regular mowing will encourage lateral spreading.

Finally, do not fertilize new lawns for at least six weeks. Then, a light fertilization of ½ pound nitrogen per 1,000 square feet is recommended. Afterward, fertilize according to the recommendations given for established lawns in Chapter 7.

Choosing the Right Grass

Don't buy seed on impulse! Choosing the right grass for your lawn can make the difference between having a low-maintenance, environmentally friendly lawn and one that is susceptible to diseases, pests, and weeds. The type of seed you choose depends on several factors. First, what do you want your lawn to look like? Grasses vary in color, leaf width, habit (characteristic appearance), and density. Second, how much time and money are you willing to spend? Higher-maintenance grasses mean greater cost and time commitments. Third, your seed choice should depend on your growing conditions: the amount of sun your site gets, soil type, its level of fertility, expected rainfall, and your climate. Finally, consider how your lawn will be used: for landscaping, erosion control, or as a play area. After considering these questions, continue reading to learn more about variations in grass growth and appearance.

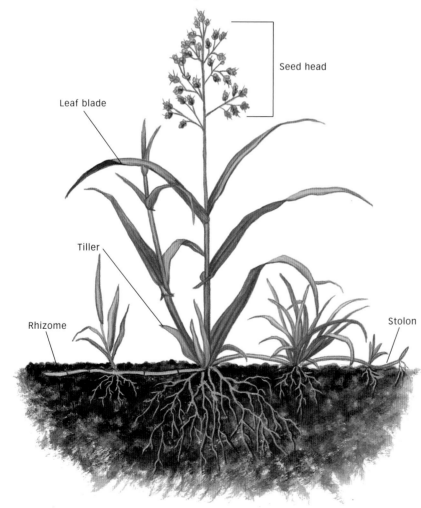

Seed head

Leaf blade

Tiller

Rhizome

Stolon

The imaginary grass plant ABOVE SHOWS FEATURES OF ALL THREE TYPES OF GRASS BEFORE GOING TO SEED: BUNCH GRASSES, STOLON-FORMING GRASSES, AND RHIZOME-FORMING GRASSES.

Basic Distinctions

Different species of grasses have distinctive growth habits that will affect the appearance of turf. Bunch grasses, such as ryegrasses and most fescues, don't spread but enlarge through the growth of sideshoots, or tillers. Bunch grasses are easy to spot if your lawn thins out because they look like small clumps or islands arising from the same crown. They wear well, but they don't form a solid sod, and you may need to overseed frequently to fill in areas where the grass dies.

Some other grasses have rhizomes, underground runners that extend out to create new plants. Kentucky bluegrass spreads this way, which is why it's planted in mixtures along with bunch grasses. Having rhizomes, it forms strong sod and is able to quickly regrow into injured areas.

■ *Grass Types*

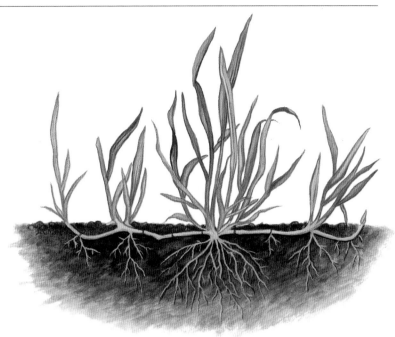

KENTUCKY BLUEGRASS AND RED FESCUES SPREAD BY A COMBINATION OF UNDERGROUND RUNNERS (RHIZOMES) AND SIDESHOOTS, OR TILLERS.

Tiller

Bunch grasses, SUCH AS RYEGRASS, TALL FESCUES, AND CRESTED WHEAT-GRASS, SPREAD BY MEANS OF TILLERS.

● ● ● ● ● ● ● ● ● ● ● ● ● ● ● ● ●

Did You Know?

There are approximately 10,000 grass species in the world. Only about 50 can make a good lawn.

Centipedegrass SPREADS BY ABOVE-GROUND RUNNERS CALLED STOLONS.

Other types of grass spread by developing new plants from aboveground runners, known as stolons. This is typical of the vigorous growth of many southern grasses, and explains why they frequently crowd out other grasses and weeds when planted in an existing lawn. Certain grasses, such as zoysia and creeping fescue, use a combination of these methods to expand. Lastly, if mature seed heads are not mowed off, some grasses are likely to spread through dispersal of their own seed.

Color, Texture, and Density

DENSITY ALSO AFFECTS APPEARANCE. DENSE TURF, ABOVE, CROWDS OUT WEEDS AND SUPPORTS TRAFFIC BETTER THAN SPARSE TURF, BELOW.

GRASS COLOR AND TEXTURE VARY BY SPECIES, AS SHOWN ABOVE, AND BY EXPOSURE TO SUN, DEGREE OF FERTILIZATION, AND IMPACT OF SUMMER DROUGHT.

Variations in Texture

A key characteristic of grass is its texture. Determined by the width of individual grass blades, texture ranges from coarse to fine. Both fine fescues and bluegrasses have narrow blades described as providing a carpet-like lawn. Bentgrass, another fine-leaved species, makes up the velvet-like greens on golf courses. Unless you want a putting green, don't try to replicate this look. The high level of care bentgrass requires makes it unsuitable for most home lawns.

A grass that is termed coarse has wider blades and doesn't necessarily wear better. Tall fescues in the North, and St. Augustine, bahiagrass, and centipedegrass in the South, are considered coarse. Just to keep things interesting, blade texture can vary by cultivar within the same species. Zoysia is a prime example: 'Emerald' is fine-textured, 'Meyer' is medium, and 'Sunrise' is coarse!

Other Important Characteristics

Color is another important characteristic of grass. There are many variations on the theme of green, from bluish gray to apple green. This wouldn't matter much except that at some point you're apt to be combining different grasses, and for the sake of uniformity, you'll be happier if they blend well. Check for color descriptions on seed labels. When in doubt, ask your Cooperative Extension Service or a local nursery manager.

Also consider a turf's density and shade tolerance. Density refers to the number of leaves or shoots growing in an area. A healthy and mature cool-season lawn averages six to eight turf plants per square inch. Finer-leaved grasses, such as fine fescues, generally produce denser and more uniform lawns in the North. In the South, Bermudagrass and zoysiagrass exhibit high-density growth.

Shade should be a major consideration in choosing grass. Fine fescue, the most shade-tolerant cool-season grass, still needs two to four hours of direct sunlight a day. Shade-tolerant grasses also require different management than sun-loving species.

Cool-Season versus Warm-Season

There is yet to be a breed of grass able to thrive on Vermont ski slopes and amid Florida orange trees. For this reason grasses are divided into two main groups, *cool-season* and *warm-season*, and divided further into two subgroups, *native* and *transitional zone*. The cool-season grasses all thrive in northern areas, including Canada, and in higher elevations farther south. Their main growth period is in spring and fall when soil temperatures are 50° to 65°F, and the air temperature is 60° to 75°F. Come high summer, they usually go dormant unless they are kept under regular irrigation. Kentucky bluegrass, bentgrass, ryegrass, and the fescues are all cool-season grasses.

Warm-season grasses grow best in southern regions and rev up their growth along with the increasing heat of summer. Growing strongly when soil temperatures are between 70° and 90°F, and the air is a balmy 80° to 95°F, they become dormant with the onset of cooler weather. The degree of tolerance of warm-season grasses varies by cultivar, but many turn straw-colored or light brown after the first frost.

• •

Did You Know? The grass at Yankee Stadium is Merion bluegrass. At Pebble Beach Golf Links, the greens are annual bluegrass (Poa annua) *and the tees and fairways are perennial ryegrass. At Augusta National Golf Club, the greens are bentgrass and the tees and fairways are Bermudagrass. The 19 courts used for Wimbledon (including Centre Court) at The All England Lawn Tennis & Croquet Club are all composed purely of perennial ryegrass.*

The Bermuda, St. Augustine, and zoysia grasses are just a few in this group. Some grasses can adapt to the climate in the band across the country where North meets South—the transitional zone. Depending on whom you ask, this zone extends from southern California, east through Oklahoma and Kansas, to the eastern coastal states of Virginia, the Carolinas, and Georgia. Tall fescues and zoysiagrass are the two grasses most frequently used in this transitional area. Native, or prairie, grasses are those adapted to the arid conditions of the Great Plains. Drought resistance and a preference for neglect are their most desirable qualities. Buffalograss, wheatgrass, and blue gamma are all native grasses that do well under these conditions.

Perennial versus Annual Grasses

The penalty for not knowing whether your grass is a perennial or an annual may be disappointment when your lawn dies out after one growing season. Given appropriate conditions, grass labeled as perennial will persist year after year. Although annual grasses generally last for just one season, they are prized for their fast and vigorous growth. This makes them a good cover crop that prevents soil erosion.

Annual grasses are also used as nurse, or companion, grasses to shade perennial grasses that have slower-growing seed. In the South, annual ryegrasses are sometimes used to overseed warm-season grasses, providing green color during the latter's winter dormancy.

Merion bluegrass is the preferred cultivar at Yankee Stadium.

Purchasing Seed

There are two ways to purchase grass seed. You can visit the garden section of a retail store and pick out a package labeled with intended use, such as "Shade Mix." Or you can buy the latest cultivars and make up your own mix. For this you will need to nose around, starting with a good nursery. If the nursery doesn't carry what you want, staff there can probably suggest where to shop. Calling the customer service departments of the large seed producers should also yield results. Either way, you will still need to know the basics about purchasing seed, beginning with the terms *species* and *cultivar*.

The word *species* refers to a group of closely related plants that differ from one another in only minor ways. Tall fescues are one species of lawn grass. The various members of a species are called varieties (which originally occurred in nature) or cultivars (variations that came about in *culti*vation, as a result of deliberate breeding). In common usage the terms *variety* and *cultivar* are often interchanged, but there is a difference between them. Grass cultivars include old standbys, such as the tall fescues 'Alta' or 'Kentucky 31', as well as new types that have been bred and chosen for superior characteristics. Newer grass cultivars, in most cases, are highly recommended.

Mixtures and Blends

Cool-season grasses are frequently packaged in either a mixture or blend. Mixtures have two or more species of grass, and blends contain two or more cultivars of the same species. There are many advantages to planting a mixture or blend. For one thing, the turf will be more resistant to diseases and pests because each cultivar or species has its own strengths and weaknesses. And because most lawns have a variety of growing conditions, the different grasses can grow where they are best adapted within your lawn.

In a typical mixture containing bluegrass, ryegrass, and fine fescue, the fescues will thrive in the shady portion of the lawn, while the bluegrass will do best in the sunny areas. If conditions should turn adverse for one of the grasses, you won't lose the entire lawn, just the part that's made up of the susceptible grass.

Smart TIP

SEED STORAGE

While unused grass seed may remain viable for years, its rate of germination will decrease over time. Be sure to keep seed stored in a cool, dry environment. To maintain optimal viability, the rule of thumb for storage is that the temperature and the relative humidity added together should be less than 100. Note: seed stored in plastic bags will be a magnet for hungry mice and other rodents looking for a place to winter over and have a free meal. Seed stored in a 5-gallon pail with a tight-fitting lid would be a better choice.

Unlike cool-season grasses, warm-season grasses tend to be planted as monostands, meaning that a single type of seed is plated, not a mixture. Their growth via stolons and rhizomes makes them so vigorous that other grasses cannot compete. Because of their distinctive appearance, some grasses, such as the original tall fescues and most native grasses, also look better planted alone.

Grass Seed Labels

Thanks to the passage of the Federal Seed Act of 1936, grass-seed labeling must meet certain requirements. This allows you to know at a glance what is in any given box, including what percentage of the seed will germinate. When you shop for seed, it pays to compare brands closely and to remember the adage, " the lawn you grow is no better than the seed you buy." The extra expense for higher-quality seed is usually worth it. Check the labels and try to avoid mixtures containing lower-quality grasses, such as timothy, meadow fescue, orchard grass, tall oatgrass, and annual ryegrass. Do not purchase seed that is identified "Variety Not Stated," or "VNS." Look also for endophyte-containing grasses and for cultivars recommended for your area by contacting your Cooperative Extension Service. (See page 87.)

Understanding Grass Labels

The grasses being bred today have numerous advantages over their older cousins. For starters, many display increased insect and disease resistance and improved drought tolerance. To reap the benefits such grasses can provide, you'll need to introduce them into your lawn through spot reseeding, lawn renovation, and planting anew. Read the grass-seed label to see whether disease- and pest-resistant cultivars are in a given box of seed.

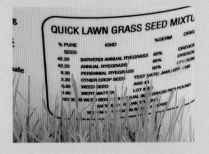

Did You Know? Plants can have a number of names. The common name, such as Kentucky bluegrass, is one with which most people are familiar. In addition, plants have a two-part botanical name. The first word, the genus, indicates a group of species that have similar structural parts. The second word, the species, indicates plants that have additional common attributes and similar methods of reproduction. Knowing that Kentucky bluegrass is also called Poa pratensis allows you to identify other plants from the same genus and species. This is because their botanical names will also include the genus, Poa, and the species, pratensis.

Blade type. Fine, narrow-leaved grasses produce attractive and more uniform lawns. Coarse grasses are better for areas that receive hard wear.

Kinds and percentages (purity). Package labels must state the name of each kind of seed present and its percentage in the mix. In high-quality seed mixtures, 80 to 100 percent of the total mix will consist of desirable permanent lawn species. The published percentages are based on weight, not the number of seeds. For example, there are approximately 500,000 fine fescue seeds per pound of grass seed and 1 million bluegrass seeds per pound. Thus, in a 50/50 bluegrass/fine fescue mixture measured by weight, only one-third of the total number of seeds is fine fescue, and the bluegrass would predominate with two-thirds of the seeds. (This is desirable because, given their vigorous nature, the fine fescue seedlings would otherwise overwhelm the bluegrass.)

Cultivar. The trade names of the varieties included in the mix and not just the generic names, such as fine fescue, should be noted on the label. When they aren't, an older variety that may not have the advantages of the improved species has probably been used.

Germination. This is the percentage of seeds expected to produce plants under favorable conditions. Look for a minimum germination rate of 75 percent for Kentucky bluegrass and 85 percent for perennial ryegrass, tall fescue, and fine fescue.

Test date. This is the date seeds were tested for germination rates. Most states consider germination percentages to be reliable for up to nine months after testing. As the seed ages, the germination rate decreases.

Weed seeds. Good-quality grass seed usually contains no more than 0.5 percent weed seeds; high-quality grass seed has none.

Noxious weeds. These are troublesome plant species that are difficult to control. Each state has its own list and amount per pound allowed. Avoid any if possible. Check with your Cooperative Extension Service for an up-to-date list of these noxious weeds for your area before purchasing seed.

Inert matter. This is dirt, chaff, and other bits that take up productive seed space. Inert matter should be no more than 5 percent. The less, the better.

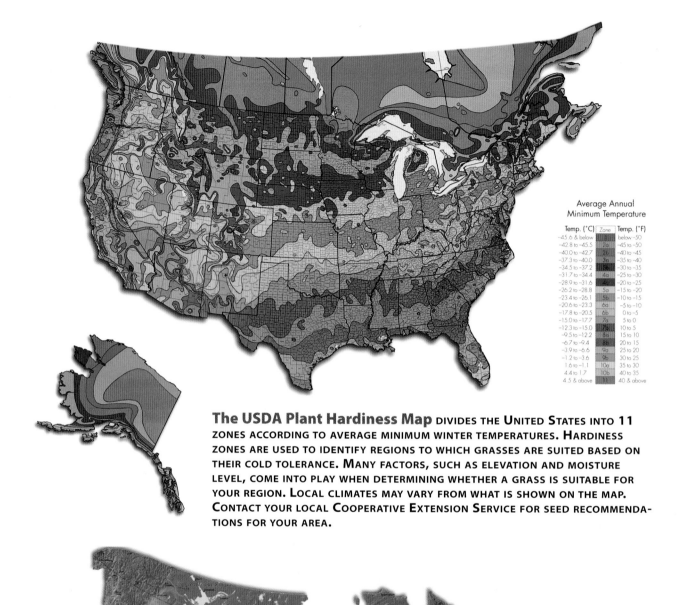

Average Annual
Minimum Temperature

Temp. (°C)	Zone	Temp. (°F)
-45.6 & below	1	below -50
-42.8 to -45.5	2a	-45 to -50
-40.0 to -42.7	2b	-40 to -45
-37.3 to -40.0	3a	-35 to -40
-34.5 to -37.2	3b	-30 to -35
-31.7 to -34.4	4a	-25 to -30
-28.9 to -31.6	4b	-20 to -25
-26.2 to -28.8	5a	-15 to -20
-23.4 to -26.1	5b	-10 to -15
-20.6 to -23.3	6a	-5 to -10
-17.8 to -20.5	6b	0 to -5
-15.0 to -17.7	7a	5 to 0
-12.3 to -15.0	7b	10 to 5
-9.5 to -12.2	8a	15 to 10
-6.7 to -9.4	8b	20 to 15
-3.9 to -6.6	9a	25 to 20
-1.2 to -3.6	9b	30 to 25
1.6 to -1.1	10a	35 to 30
4.4 to 1.7	10b	40 to 35
4.5 & above	11	40 & above

The USDA Plant Hardiness Map DIVIDES THE UNITED STATES INTO 11 ZONES ACCORDING TO AVERAGE MINIMUM WINTER TEMPERATURES. HARDINESS ZONES ARE USED TO IDENTIFY REGIONS TO WHICH GRASSES ARE SUITED BASED ON THEIR COLD TOLERANCE. MANY FACTORS, SUCH AS ELEVATION AND MOISTURE LEVEL, COME INTO PLAY WHEN DETERMINING WHETHER A GRASS IS SUITABLE FOR YOUR REGION. LOCAL CLIMATES MAY VARY FROM WHAT IS SHOWN ON THE MAP. CONTACT YOUR LOCAL COOPERATIVE EXTENSION SERVICE FOR SEED RECOMMENDATIONS FOR YOUR AREA.

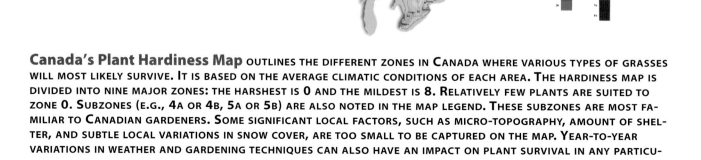

Plant Hardiness Zones

Canada's Plant Hardiness Map OUTLINES THE DIFFERENT ZONES IN CANADA WHERE VARIOUS TYPES OF GRASSES WILL MOST LIKELY SURVIVE. IT IS BASED ON THE AVERAGE CLIMATIC CONDITIONS OF EACH AREA. THE HARDINESS MAP IS DIVIDED INTO NINE MAJOR ZONES: THE HARSHEST IS **0** AND THE MILDEST IS **8**. RELATIVELY FEW PLANTS ARE SUITED TO ZONE **0**. SUBZONES (E.G., **4A** OR **4B**, **5A** OR **5B**) ARE ALSO NOTED IN THE MAP LEGEND. THESE SUBZONES ARE MOST FAMILIAR TO CANADIAN GARDENERS. SOME SIGNIFICANT LOCAL FACTORS, SUCH AS MICRO-TOPOGRAPHY, AMOUNT OF SHELTER, AND SUBTLE LOCAL VARIATIONS IN SNOW COVER, ARE TOO SMALL TO BE CAPTURED ON THE MAP. YEAR-TO-YEAR VARIATIONS IN WEATHER AND GARDENING TECHNIQUES CAN ALSO HAVE AN IMPACT ON PLANT SURVIVAL IN ANY PARTICU-

Which Grass Where?

If you read the research reports from various grass institutes, you will be astonished by the number of cultivars of grass species. When you throw into the mix the numerous characteristics of each grass and how each grows under different conditions, the task of selecting the best for your location and intended use can seem daunting. Avoid confusion by contacting your Cooperative Extension Service and speaking with a turfgrass specialist. Other excellent resources are the National Turfgrass Evaluation Program (NTEP) and the Guelph Turfgrass Institute in Ontario, Canada. See the Resource Guide, page 168, for contact information.

If you choose to do the research on your own, start by using the Plant Hardiness Maps on the previous page to find out in which zone you live. A grass that's right for Vermont may not fare well in Texas. You can also check the cultivars listed at the end of each description on the following pages. There are two sections, one for warm-season grasses and one for cool-season grasses. They are just a few of those generally recognized to have outstanding characteristics for their species. Whether they are appropriate choices for your lawn depends on the growing environment where you live. With ongoing research, new, improved cultivars are regularly being introduced.

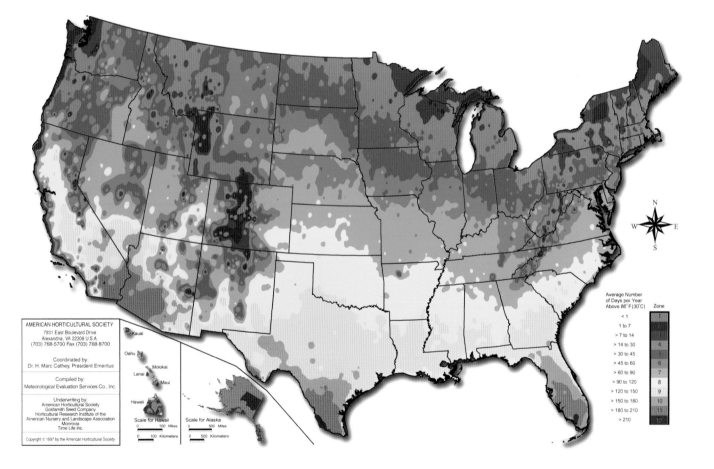

The American Horticultural Society Heat-Zone Map DIVIDES THE UNITED STATES INTO 12 ZONES BASED ON THE AVERAGE ANNUAL NUMBER OF DAYS A REGION'S TEMPERATURES CLIMB ABOVE 86°F, THE TEMPERATURE AT WHICH THE CELLULAR PROTEINS OF PLANTS BEGIN TO EXPERIENCE INJURY. INTRODUCED IN 1998, THE MAP IS ESPECIALLY HELPFUL FOR GARDENERS IN SOUTHERN AND TRANSITIONAL ZONES. NURSERIES, GROWERS, AND OTHER PLANT SOURCES LIST BOTH COLD HARDINESS AND HEAT TOLERANCE ZONES FOR PLANTS, INCLUDING GRASS PLANTS. USING THE USDA PLANT HARDINESS MAP, WHICH CAN HELP DETERMINE A PLANT'S COLD TOLERANCE, AND THE AHS HEAT-ZONE MAP, GARDENERS CAN SAFELY CHOOSE GRASSES THAT TOLERATE THEIR REGION'S LOWEST AND HIGHEST TEMPERATURES.

Cool-Season Grasses

Kentucky Bluegrass (Poa pratensis)

Kentucky bluegrass fits the bill if you want a deep green, fine-textured, attractive lawn. Able to take moisture and temperature extremes, bluegrass is winter hardy and will grow in full sun to light shade depending on cultivar and location. Sown by seed and spread by rhizomes and tillers, it forms strong, dense sod that recovers well from injury. Maintenance requirements vary, with some of the older common cultivars requiring less water, nutrients, and care, but they are highly susceptible to leaf spot and other diseases. Newer, more maintenance-intensive cultivars grow aggressively, crowding out weeds and showing increased resistance to pests and diseases.

Drawbacks: It's slow to germinate, and during prolonged hot, dry weather, Kentucky bluegrass goes dormant, losing its color. Performs poorly in wet soils or shade.

Recommendations: For USDA Hardiness Zones 2 to 7. When planting a bluegrass lawn, blend at least three varieties to take advantage of differing disease and pest resistances. Generally speaking, look for improved bluegrasses such as 'Everglade', 'Midnight', 'Nu-Glade', 'Starburst', and 'Bewitched'. 'Everest', 'Excursion', and 'Midnight' can tolerate traffic well; 'Everest', 'Bar VV', and 'Midnight' are tolerant of heat and drought. With more than 100 cultivars to choose from, consult a local nursery or your local Cooperative Extension Service to find the best choice for your locale.

Rough-stalked bluegrass (Poa trivialis)

This moderately fine-textured, light-to-medium-green grass spreads by weak stolons. New seedlings are vigorous, tolerating acid soils as well as poorly drained, moist, shaded sites. Not minding low temperatures, rough-stalked bluegrass keeps its color well into the fall. It's best in low-traffic areas.

Drawbacks: With shallow roots, rough-stalked bluegrass cannot tolerate hot, dry conditions.

Recommendations: For USDA Hardiness Zones 4 to 7. Plant in moist shade. Look for 'Sabre II', 'Cypress', and 'Stardust'.

Cool-Season Grasses

KENTUCKY BLUE-GRASS IS THE MOST WIDELY USED COOL-SEASON SPECIES AND THE ALL-AROUND BEST CHOICE FOR GENERAL LAWN PURPOSES.

ROUGH-STALKED BLUEGRASS LIKES MOIST, SHADY CONDITIONS AND BECOMES PATCHY IN SUNNY AREAS.

TALL FESCUE IS A GOOD CHOICE FOR SUNNY LAWNS AND PLAYGROUNDS IN THE NORTH AND TRANSITIONAL ZONES.

FINE FESCUES ARE IDEAL FOR SHADED, LOW-MAINTENANCE LAWNS. THEY MIX WELL WITH BLUE-GRASSES AND PERENNIAL RYE-GRASS.

PERENNIAL RYE-GRASS GERMI-NATES RAPIDLY, WEARS WELL, AND IS FREQUENTLY FOUND IN SEED MIXTURES.

Tall fescue (Festuca arundinacea)

Having a deep root system that enables it to tolerate drought and heat, tall fescue has been used for years as a durable utility grass. The older, wide-bladed forage types are no longer considered good choices for lawns. Choose improved tall fescues known as "turf-type." These denser, finer-leaved, darker turf-types have the advantage of being more resistant to diseases and insects.

Drawbacks: In far northern regions and areas of shade, tall fescues are prone to thin out and form clumps, causing the lawn to require overseeding. A bunchgrass with minimal rhizomes, tall fescue makes a fairly weak sod that is slow to recover from injury, but the grass itself wears well.

Recommendations: For USDA Hardiness Zones 2 to 7. Consider stress-resistant types, such as 'Cayenne', '2nd Millennium', and 'Rebel Exeda', according to the NTEP rankings.

Fine fescue (Festuca species)

While genetically different, species in this genus—chewings, creeping red, and hard fescue—share some similar characteristics. They are fine textured and dark green, making them mix well with bluegrasses and perennial rye. Forming a dense, upright, good-looking turf, all grow well in acidic soils and shade. These three are the most drought and shade tolerant of the cool-season grasses, and they don't require much fertilizer. Many fescues are also endophyte-enhanced and, when added to other grasses, increase both their disease and pest resistance. Except for creeping fescue, which has rhizomes, fescues are bunch grasses.

Drawbacks: Fescues need well-drained soil and don't stand up well to heat or heavy wear.

Recommendations: For USDA Hardiness Zones 2 to 7. Fine fescues are usually found in shade mixtures. Consider '7 Seas,' 'Ambassador,' 'Audubon,' and 'Berkshire'. Dollar spot-resistant cultivars include 'Cardinal', 'Epic', 'Garnet', 'Pathfinder', and 'Ambassador', according to the NTEP rankings.

Perennial ryegrass (Lolium perenne)

A bright green bunchgrass with a fine to medium texture, perennial ryegrass grows well in a wide range of soils, even wet soils. Having finer, denser, darker green leaves, the improved low-growth turf-types are replacing older varieties. Many of the new cultivars are also endophyte-enhanced for improved disease- and pest-resistance. Ryegrasses withstand foot traffic and compacted soils. Starting quickly from seed, they make excellent "nurse" grasses, protecting slower-growing species, and are used to overseed warm-season lawns. They do best in coastal regions with mild winters and cool, moist summers.

Drawbacks: Perennial ryegrasses, especially older varieties, have a low tolerance for drought and cold and are prone to pythium blight. They are best in mixtures but should not make up more than 20 percent because they grow so vigorously.

Recommendations: For USDA Hardiness Zones 3 to 7. Look for highly ranked NTEP cultivars, such as 'Saturn II', 'Manhattan 3', 'Blackhawk', and 'SR 4200'.

Warm-Season Grasses

St. Augustinegrass (Stenotaphrum secundatum)

Easily grown from sod, plugs, or sprigs, St. Augustinegrass produces a dense blue-green turf that has good shade and salt tolerance. It is highly popular in coastal areas from Florida to California.

Drawbacks: St. Augustinegrass will produce thick thatch if heavily fertilized and watered. It is vulnerable to chinch bugs and grubs, and it's texture is somewhat coarse.

Recommendations: For USDA Hardiness Zones 8 to 10. Look for slow-growing 'Amerishade', cold- and shade-tolerant 'Classic', and chinch bug-resistant 'Floratam', according to the NTEP.

Zoysiagrass (Zoysia species)

Popular in the transitional zone and the South, Zoysiagrass was once touted as a miracle grass because of its especially thick, slow-growing turf. While it may take two years to establish, you'll end up with a lawn that weeds can rarely penetrate. Having a fine-to-medium texture, its color varies by cultivar. Being deep-rooted and fibrous, it doesn't mind heat or drought, although it does need an oc-

Warm-Season Grasses

ST. AUGUSTINE GRASS, DESPITE ITS COARSE LEAVES, IS FAVORED IN WARM, HUMID CLIMATES FOR ITS ABILITY TO TOLERATE SHADE AND SALT.

ZOYSIAGRASS PROVIDES ONE OF THE MOST UNIFORM AND DENSE LAWNS POSSIBLE, BUT IT HAS A STRAW-LIKE APPEARANCE IN WINTER.

BERMUDAGRASS IS GOOD FOR SUNNY SOUTHERN LAWNS THAT RECEIVE HEAVY USE, BUT IT IS INVASIVE AND REQUIRES EDGING.

CENTIPEDEGRASS IS A SLOW-GROWING OPTION FOR SOUTHERN SOILS WITH LOW FERTILITY, BUT IT DOESN'T BEAR UP WELL UNDER HEAVY USE.

BAHIAGRASS, BECAUSE OF ITS DEEP ROOTS, GROWS WELL IN HOT CLIMATES ON INFERTILE, DRY SOILS. IT IS, HOWEVER, COARSE AND DIFFICULT TO MOW.

CARPETGRASS GROWS IN WET, POORLY DRAINED SOUTHERN SOILS WHERE OTHER GRASSES WILL NOT.

casional watering. Zoysia is winter hardy and isn't particular about soil. It also copes well with salt spray, pests, diseases, and some shade.

Drawbacks: The main complaint about zoysia is its unrelenting straw color in the fall. Furthermore, the characteristics that make zoysia so durable also make it prone to thatch and difficult to mow. Add poor recuperative powers and high fertility needs, and you have a high-maintenance turf.

Recommendations: For USDA Hardiness Zones 6 to 9. There are several species of zoysia to choose from. *Zoysia japonica*, known as Japanese lawn grass, with its coarse, light green leaves is the best choice for colder climates. *Zoysia matrella*, also called Manilagrass, is a less winter-hardy, slower-growing species that creates a denser, finer lawn. 'Zorro' and 'Emerald' are top-ranked cultivars according to NTEP tests.

Bermudagrass (Cynodon *species*)

One of the most widely used southern grasses, Bermudagrass thrives on numerous soil types, even salty soils. With a deep root system, it takes sun, heat, and dry conditions in stride, forming a strong, erosion-resistant sod. Having both rhizomes and stolons, Bermudagrass quickly fills in damaged areas with its generally fine, low growth. New hybrids, some growing from seed, show improved color, texture, disease resistance, and cold tolerance. They cost less to maintain and establish quickly.

Drawbacks: Bermudagrass requires edging to prevent invasive growth; it also forms thatch and generally requires intensive management. Needing full sun, it's the least shade-tolerant of southern grasses. It also turns a straw-like brown after a frost, making it a candidate for winter overseeding.

Recommendations: For USDA Hardiness Zones 7 to 10. Look for improved cultivars, such as 'Tifsport', 'Tifway', 'Aussie Green', 'Celebration', 'Premier', and 'Patriot'. If frost is a worry, 'Tifsport', 'Tifway', and 'Ashmore' are the most tolerant.

Centipedegrass (Eremochloa ophiuroides)

Growing in full sun to partial shade, this apple-green grass prefers well-drained acid soils. It can be grown from seed, and is known for its slow rate of growth, which means it requires less mowing. A low-maintenance warm-season grass, it spreads by stolons, forming a moderately dense low-growth turf of medium-textured grass.

Drawbacks: Centipedegrass doesn't bear up well under heavy use. Salt spray poses problems, as does a lack of iron, which leads to yellowing. Avoid using excess amounts of fertilizer, which fosters heavy thatch development that leads to large brown dead patches.

Recommendations: For USDA Hardiness Zones 7 to 8. Cultivars with better cold tolerance, such as 'Oklawn' and 'Centennial', are available.

Bahiagrass (Paspalum notatum)

An up-and-comer for low-upkeep home lawns, bahiagrass grows from seed and forms an apple-green lawn with a relatively open growth habit. Having gotten its start as a pasture grass on infertile, sandy soils, it has a prolific root system enabling it to withstand drought. It also forms a durable wear-resistant sod, and most pests leave it alone.

Drawbacks: Bahiagrass is coarse, making it tough to mow. Some people object to the look of its tall seed heads and light green color. It may yellow from lack of iron and grows poorly in alkaline soils and in areas with salt spray.

Recommendations: For USDA Hardiness Zones 7 to 10. Avoid common bahiagrass; 'Argentine', 'Tifton 9', and 'Pensacola' are the preferred cultivars.

Carpetgrass (Axonopus affinis)

Not minding some shade and preferring wet feet, carpetgrass will grow where few others can. Similar to centipedegrass, with its apple-green color and medium-wide blades, carpetgrass is spread by creeping stolons and can be grown from seed. While it won't yield a high-quality lawn, it provides an alternative for boggy sites in warm climates.

Drawbacks: With shallow roots and no rhizomes, carpetgrass needs watering when dry and won't stand up to wear. It's also quick to brown-out in the fall and slow to green-up in the spring.

Recommendations: For USDA Hardiness Zones 8 to 9. No named varieties are available, so look for the species *Axonopus Affinis*.

Native Grasses

BUFFALOGRASS THRIVES IN HOT, DRY CLIMATES AND ONLY OCCASIONALLY NEEDS WATERING OR MOWING. IT RARELY NEEDS FERTILIZING, AND FEW PEST FEED ON IT.

BLUE GRAMA IS A TOUGH GRASS THAT WEARS WELL UNDER HEAVY USE AND TOLERATES HEAT, DROUGHT, AND COLD. IT REQUIRES LITTLE MOWING.

AS WITH ALL PRAIRIE GRASSES, CRESTED WHEAT-GRASS REQUIRES LITTLE UPKEEP. IT THRIVES IN COOL, SEMIARID CONDITIONS AND NEEDS FEW WATERINGS BECAUSE OF ITS DEEP ROOT SYSTEM.

Native Grasses

Having evolved on and adapted to the arid grassland plains, these grasses are survivors. They require little maintenance and provide a grass cover that is more open and natural in appearance than traditional turfgrasses. Native grasses grow best during the hot summer months and prefer full sun. They are widely adapted to areas across the United States and Canada and are especially suited to the grasslands of the Central Plains states. Check with your local Cooperative Extension Service to learn whether native grasses are suitable for your region.

Buffalograss (Buchloe dactyloides)

Coming from the Great Plains, where water efficiency is a necessity, buffalograss is resistant to heat and drought. It tolerates cool temperatures better than most warm-season grasses, and keeps its color into the fall. Often grown from seed, it spreads slowly by stolons and self-sown seeds to form a gray-green, fine-textured lawn that attains a height of 4 to 5 inches. Best in full sun, it prefers well-drained loam and abhors wet, poorly drained, or sandy soils. Depending on rainfall, it may still need an occasional watering to prevent summer dormancy, but far less than other grasses. Because it grows slowly, buffalograss needs only several mowings a season. Its sparse appearance is not for everyone, and it doesn't do as well in humid regions, such as Florida. It has few pest problems, but white grubs, webworms, and chinch bugs do feed on it. When buying, look for improved cultivars, such as '609', 'Density', '378', 'Bowie', and 'Legacy'.

Alkaligrass (Puccinellia distans)

With its high tolerance to saline (salty) soils, alkaligrass is recommended along the coastal seaboards of New England, in the Mid-Atlantic, and along the West Coast. This slow-growing, finely textured, blue-green bunch grass is also adapted to cool, temperate inland regions that have moderately hot summers. It has excellent cold hardiness and keeps its color well into the fall. The upright, dense growth can be kept mowed at 3 inches or left to attain its natural height of 12 to 16 inches. It does best in full-sun locations with adequate moisture and little traffic. Look for cultivars or mixtures developed for use in wetlands and along shorelines if you live near the water.

Blue grama (Bouteloua gracilis)

Blue grama grows well from seed or plugs, and forms a gray-green, low-growth turf that spreads slowly by rhizomes. Having a fibrous root system, it forms strong sod and is quite tolerant of heat and drought, although it will turn brown and go dormant. It tolerates low temperatures but is slow to green-up in the spring. It's better adapted to both sandy and fine soils than buffalograss because it tolerates alkaline conditions. In arid areas, blue grama is frequently mixed with buffalograss for a low-maintenance lawn that needs little mowing. Its seed heads and small flowers make it an interesting choice for naturalistic areas.

Crested wheatgrass (Agropyron cristatum)

Frequently used along roadways and for lawns planted on dry lands, this hardy cool-season bunch grass produces long, coarse, medium-green tapered foliage that is well adapted to cool, semiarid conditions. In states such as Wyoming, where yearly rainfall may range from 8 to 15 inches, crested wheatgrass thrives, thanks to its especially deep root system. It develops flat, cockscomb-like seed heads and will become partially dormant during hot spells. As with other prairie grasses, it doesn't require much mowing or other upkeep. 'Fairway' is the preferred cultivar—it is leafier and finer textured than common crested wheatgrass.

Endophytes: Nature's Repellents

Endophytes are small fungi that live in some grasses and make them harmful or deadly to a variety of grass-eating insects. Discovered by scientists in New Zealand who observed that cattle got sick after eating certain grasses, endophytes have opened a new frontier in grass research. Because endophytes live primarily in the lower stem and crown of grass plants, surface pests such as sod webworms, armyworms, billbugs, cutworms, and chinch bugs are deterred, but not underground pests such as white grubs, which feed on roots.

Endophytic fungi get their start in turf by infecting the grass seed. Harmless to children or pets that may occasionally eat the grass, and to the grass itself, the fungi remain inside the growing plant. New seed produced by infected plants will also contain these important fungi, but unfortunately, it's not currently possible to introduce endophytes separately into established lawns.

Ongoing research is focused on finding ways to insert endophytes into different grasses. When buying seed, check to see whether any endophyte grasses are listed on the label. Endophytes do not stay viable in unused seed for long, so store seed in a cool place and use it within nine months of the test date. Contact your local Cooperative Extension Service for more information on endophytes.

Overseeding Southern Lawns for Winter Color

Warm-season grasses have a major drawback for homeowners: their color disappears when winter arrives. To have green grass in winter, some southerners overseed their lawns, using fine fescue, bluegrass, or ryegrass. These cool-season grasses find a hospitable habitat among the dormant southern grasses and then die off with the return of warm weather in the spring. Aside from improved aesthetics, overseeding helps prevent the establishment of winter weeds, but it may also slow your permanent turf's spring green-up.

Do not overseed until daytime temperatures get down to the low to mid 70s and your permanent lawn grass has gone dormant. To prepare for overseeding, rake off any debris; mow the lawn closely; and dethatch if needed.

Use a spreader to overseed, sowing half in one direction and the other half at a right angle to the first. Then rake the lawn briskly to help move the seed down to the soil. Finish off with a light watering and continue to water daily until the seedlings are well established.

Maintaining the grass over the winter will require monthly feeding. The temporary winter grass should not be encouraged once spring approaches, so stop fertilizing, water infrequently, and mow closely until the permanent grass resumes growth.

PART 2

MAKING LAWN CARE EASIER

Choosing a Mower

For more than 150 years, yards and gardens have become progressively more mechanized. Human- and animal-powered machines have gradually given way to compact equipment powered by internal combustion engines of all sizes and configurations. Nevertheless, homeowners still have a basic choice: power and speed or muscle and patience—with lots of permutations in between. When it comes to lawn mowers, equipment that nearly every homeowner needs, the choices range from manual reel push mowers to technologically sophisticated zero-turn-radius mowers. Power and speed, of course, come at a price. At the high end, you can spend $12,000 or more; at the low end, less than $150. Most homeowners find they can satisfy their needs with an investment of $300 to $2,500. To begin your search, review the categories of mowing machines described in this chapter.

Walk-behind mowers with a bagging option are great when it's necessary to keep clippings from areas such as pools and outdoor kitchens.

Garden Tractors

Garden tractors cost $3,000 to $12,000, and that's without the attachments. They come with big OHV (overhead valve) engines, 20 horsepower and up. Mowing decks are up to 54 inches wide and have two or three blades. Top-of-the-line units have features such as power steering, automatic transmission, cruise control, and four-wheel drive. They can attain speeds of 9 mph, and collection bags hold up to 17 bushels. In addition to mowing, garden tractors can readily handle a host of other tasks, including lifting, tilling, aerating, spreading, hauling, and snow plowing. With 28- to 55-inch turning radii, the biggest drawback to garden tractors is maneuverability. (See "Zero-Turn-Radius Mowers," page 93, for that.)

Speed versus Utility

A ZERO-TURN-RADIUS RIDER, ABOVE, MOVES ACROSS THE GROUND FASTER THAN A LAWN TRACTOR, TOP, (ABOUT **6.5** MPH COMPARED WITH ABOUT **5** MPH) BUT STILL GIVES A CLEAN CUT THANKS TO A HIGHER BLADE-TIP SPEED (ABOUT **18,000** FEET PER MINUTE VERSUS **12,000**). IT CAN ALSO MAKE TIGHT TURNS WITHOUT THE OPERATOR NEEDING TO BACK UP AND MAKE MULTIPLE PASSES. ALL THIS GROUND SPEED AND MANEUVERABILITY TRANSLATES INTO TIME SAVED. LAWN TRACTORS, ON THE OTHER HAND, HAVE FAMILIAR STEERING CONTROLS, ACCEPT A VARIETY OF ATTACHMENTS, AND ARE MORE STABLE ON HILLY TERRAIN THAN ZERO-TURN-RADIUS MOWERS. THEY ARE A GREAT CHOICE IF YOUR LANDSCAPE IS NOT TOO COMPLEX.

Lawn Tractors

Next in the power parade are lawn tractors. Generally powered by engines with less than 20 horsepower, their mowing speeds and deck sizes are smaller (38 to 50 inches). These machines are primarily made for mowing, but those with PTO (power takeoff) can run snow throwers and push or pull nonpowered attachments, such as dethatchers and carts. Prices range from $1,500 to $5,000. The turning radius for these mowing machines can be as little as 14 inches.

Riding Mowers

Conventional residential riding mowers are generally limited to mowing. They range from small and relatively inexpensive models to large commercial-grade machines that will rival lawn tractors in cutting capability. You can get a 13.5-horsepower, 30-inch deck riding mower for about $1,200—or you can opt for a model with a 20-horsepower engine and a 44-inch mowing deck for more than twice that price.

Did You Know?

An English engineer named Edwin Budding invented the reel mower in 1830. He was inspired by a machine in a textile mill that was used to shear the nap of velvet. Power Specialties of England invented the gas-powered lawn mower in 1933.

Zero-Turn Mowers Save Time

THE HIGHLY MANEU-
VERABLE ZERO-TURN-
RADIUS MOWER GETS
THE JOB DONE FASTER
—GENERALLY AT LEAST
15 TO 50 PERCENT
FASTER THAN A LAWN
TRACTOR. THE MORE
COMPLEX THE LAND-
SCAPE, THE MORE TIME
YOU WILL SAVE.
IN ADDITION TO MA-
NEUVERING AROUND
TIGHT SPOTS, ZERO-
TURNS HAVE SUPERIOR
VISIBILITY OUT FRONT.

TO CONTROL GROUND SPEED AND DIRECTION, YOU USE
HIGHLY RESPONSIVE LEVER CONTROLS INSTEAD OF FOOT
PEDALS AND A STEERING WHEEL. BASICALLY, YOU DRIVE IT
LIKE A GROCERY CART. PUSH MORE ON THE RIGHT AND
YOU TURN LEFT. PULL BACK ON THE LEFT AT THE SAME
TIME, AS SHOWN IN THIS MOWING SEQUENCE, AND YOU
TURN 360 DEG. IN A COUNTERCLOCKWISE DIRECTION.
CLOSE CUTTING IS DONE TO THE LEFT, WHERE THE DIS-
CHARGE CHUTE IS NOT IN THE WAY.

Zero-Turn-Radius Mowers

Super-maneuverable zero-turn-radius mowers are the fastest-growing category of riding mower today. They range in price from just under $3,000 to almost $6,000—but they will reduce mowing time significantly. Zero-turn riders can turn on a dime thanks to independent rear-wheel drives (hydraulically operated transaxles or wheel motors) and caster-style wheels on the front. You can cut tight contours, such as around trees and garden beds, without having to reverse. Zero-turns have a safety advantage over tractors, too, because there is nothing in front to obstruct your view.

Zero-turn-radius riders are typically used for grass cutting only, while tractors, especially garden tractors, are more versatile. Most manufacturers offer few, if any, accessories beyond a grass collector and tow-behind trailer. Commercial models, on the other hand, can be equipped with a wide range of accessories, in part because of tougher transmissions and beefier wheel motors, and because professionals are more likely to know how to use them properly. If you buy a zero-turn-radius mower that straddles the line between residential and commercial, you may find more accessories are available, including utility carts (with caster wheels), a snow blower, a sweeper, and several types of grass collectors.

HILL HAZARDS

Smart Tip

If you have a lawn that slopes, mow up and down when using a riding mower, not side to side. Whenever possible, go around a hill and mow down the slope. With a walk-behind mower, walk behind the mower across the hill, not up and down. Don't mow on a hill with any mower when the grass is damp or wet. When in doubt, check the safety section in your owner's manual. If you have a yard with slopes greater than 15 degrees, don't use a riding mower. Consider planting the area with a ground cover or trees, or create terraced beds instead.

When using a riding mower on a slope, mow up and down, as the pattern in this lawn shows.

Buying a Zero-Turn-Radius Mower

There are significant differences in performance between zero-turn-radius models costing less than $3,000 and those costing twice that much, and an even greater difference as you move from residential into commercial models. We all have to draw lines somewhere, but your best bet usually is to buy the best mower you can afford. Knowing what makes a quality machine will make you a smarter buyer. The most important factors that determine durability are overall sturdiness of the frame and deck construction, the quality of the motor, and the load capacity of the drive system. With lower maintenance costs and a longer life span, the total annual cost of a higher-quality machine will often be less than that of a less-expensive machine.

The relative sturdiness of zero-turn-radius mowers will be immediately evident in a side-by-side inspection, but you can also compare specifications such as tubular-steel frame dimensions and the gauge of steel (the lower the gauge number, the thicker the material). Some models offer considerably better protection for the motors than others.

Commercial-grade mowers typically have fabricated decks, which are made with commercial-grade pieces of heavy gauge steel continuously welded. Many residential models have stamped decks, which are made by forming lighter-gauge steel in a press. Some decks combine both stamping and welding and approach the durability of a true fabricated deck. Anti-scalping wheels—small wheels that raise the deck when they contact a bump to prevent the blades from contacting the ground (scalping)—are common on decks 48 inches or wider, but the better ones also have a center roller, and two of the wheels may be adjustable.

Most stamped decks on zero-turn-radius mowers are the same height on the left and right. A tunnel design maximizes efficiency by tapering the deck so that it is taller on the discharge side, where the volume of clippings cut by three blades is the greatest. That translates into finer mulching and side-discharged clippings or more efficient bagging.

Twin-cylinder OHV engines, widely used on zero-turn-radius mowers, are more powerful, run smoother (less vibration), and are more durable than single-cylinder models. Don't place too much value on horsepower ratings, which range from 15 to 24. Manufacturers size horsepower appropriately for the model and cutting deck. As for engine brand, you only need to look to commercial mowers to know what engines are the most durable.

Did You Know?

On April 17, 2007, the U.S. Environmental Protection Agency, in an effort to bring emissions cuts to the United States, announced a proposal that sets strict standards for most lawn and garden equipment. Under the proposal, manufacturers will use catalytic converters for the first time on lawn and garden equipment. Catalytic converters will allow equipment to adhere to the new exhaust emissions standards. The proposed regulations would apply as early as 2011 for lawn and garden equipment under 25 horsepower. There are also regulations for larger lawn and garden equipment.

What to Look For

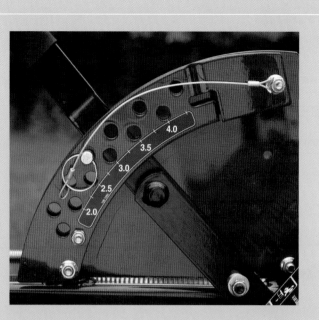

OPT FOR OVERHEAD VALVE (**OHV**) OR OVERHEAD CAM (**OHC**) ENGINE DESIGNS TO MINIMIZE VIBRATION AND NOISE. YOU ONLY NEED TO LOOK AT THE ENGINE BRANDS ON PROFESSIONAL EQUIPMENT TO KNOW WHICH CONSUMER-MODEL ENGINES ARE LIKELY TO BE DURABLE.

CHOOSE A MODEL THAT ALLOWS YOU TO EASILY RAISE THE DECK TO AVOID A TREE ROOT OR OTHER HIGH SPOT AND AUTOMATICALLY RETURN TO THE DESIRED SETTING BY RELEASING THE HAND- OR FOOT-CONTROLLED HEIGHT-OF-CUT LEVER. ON THIS MODEL, A REMOVABLE PIN SETS CUTTING HEIGHT. IN THIS CASE, THAT'S $2^3/_4$ IN.

LOOK FOR ANTI-SCALPING WHEELS MOUNTED TO THE DECK. THESE WHEELS PREVENT CONTACT WITH THE GROUND (SCALPING) WHEN PASSING OVER A HIGH SPOT.

WITH THE MANEUVERABILITY OF ZERO-TURN-RADIUS MOWERS, THE REAR ENGINE IS VULNERABLE TO DAMAGE. LOOK FOR A MODEL WITH A SOLID FRAME.

IF YOUR LAWN HAS SOME ROUGH PATCHES WITH STONES AND STUMPS, OPT FOR A RUGGED DECK. THIS ONE IS REINFORCED WITH A WELDED-ON STEEL BAR.

Perhaps the most popular accessory for a lawn tractor is a grass catcher (bagger). Be sure it's easy to use. This one is lightweight and very easy to install (or remove). Just drop the attachment's pipe into the receiving hole on the mower; rotate the unit into position; and hook the elastic strap onto the discharge chute.

Terms You Should Know

Deck: In a rotary mower, the deck is housing that covers the blade. It's an integral part of a walk-behind mower (supporting the engine, axles, and so forth) and is the primary if not sole accessory on riding mowers. It can be designed to discharge (a standard or broadcast deck), mulch (a mulching deck), or direct clippings to a collector (a bag or hard-shell compartment) from either the side or rear of the deck.

Deck Lift or Height of Cut: The system that allows you to change the cutting height. Most are spring assisted and are operated by hand or foot.

Fabricated Deck: This type of mowing deck is made by welding separate pieces of formed steel together. The steel is a heavier gauge, so this deck is more durable than a deck stamped from a sheet of metal.

Horsepower (hp): A measure of the power of an engine. Most push mowers have between 4.0 and 6.5 hp. All are adequate for small, relatively flat lawns that push mowers typically cut.

Hydrostatic Transmission: A variable-speed fluid drive transmission that does not require shifting.

Mowing Deck: The business end of the cutting machine that houses the blade or blades.

Mulching: The process of cutting and recutting clippings into fine particles, enabling them to fall back into the turf, where they quickly decompose and restore nutrients and water to the soil.

Mulch Kit: A mulching blade and, as needed, a mulch plug, which is an insert that covers a discharge opening and maintains the circular shape on the underside of the deck when a mower is being used in the mulching mode.

OHV (overhead valve): A superior engine technology that offers more power, better fuel efficiency, lower emissions, and greater durability.

PTO (power takeoff): The point(s) of attachment for mower blades and other powered attachments found on riding mower and tractors. PTO controls on late-model zero-turn-radius mowers are electric.

Scalping: Accidental damage to the turf caused by the blades coming into direct contact with a high spot. Anti-scalping wheels and rollers fitted on the mowing deck prevent or at least limit the chance of this happening by keeping the deck a minimum height above the turf.

Turning Radius: Half the diameter of an uncut circle when mowing with the wheels turned the maximum amount.

Hydraulic pumps and wheel motors originally drove all zero-turn-radius mowers—a very reliable setup that commercial models still use. Today, almost all residential zero-turn riders use integrated transaxles. The hydraulic pump and motor are in single, sealed (non-serviceable) housing, which is a less-complex and less-expensive option. The quality of these components varies, with mower manufacturers matching them to the quality, size, and price of the mower.

The cutting height should be easy to adjust. A foot assist is easier than a hand lever and also allows you to quickly and momentarily raise the deck over an exposed tree root or the like without taking a hand off the drive levers. Avoid units where you have to get off the machine and turn an awkward crank to raise and lower the deck.

Wider tires offer better traction, and four-ply rated tires are more durable than two-ply ones. Tire sizes are determined by the load rating on the axles in the transmission and are defined by three numbers (18 x 9.5 x 8, for example) representing the diameter, width, and wheel size, but often by only the diameter and width because these are the most relevant.

The little things make a difference, too. Compare seat comfort and the ease of adjustment, which is important when there's more than one user. Is the control panel easy to see and reach from your seat? Is there an hour meter? Having one makes it easier to follow a recommended maintenance schedule that is based on hours of operation. Examine the air filter—more pleats mean a larger surface area, and that means better filtering. If accessorizing is important to you, make sure the manufacturer recommends or sells the accessories you want before you buy the mower.

Riding Mower Maintenance Basics

Use your equipment's hour meter TO TRACK WHEN ROUTINE SERVICE, SUCH AS OIL CHANGES AND SPARK-PLUG REPLACEMENT, SHOULD BE PERFORMED.

Remove a deck PER YOUR MANUAL'S INSTRUCTIONS TO CHANGE BLADES, INSPECT AND REPLACE DRIVE BELTS, OR CLEAN THE UNDERSIDE OF YOUR MOWING DECK.

To remove blades, BLOCK WITH SCRAP WOOD, AND USE A SOCKET WRENCH TO REMOVE THE MOUNTING BOLT. HAVE BLADES SHARPENED AND BALANCED BY A PRO.

To replace a worn drive belt, REMOVE THE DECK AND ANY HOUSING. THERE IS NO TENSION ON THE BELT AT THIS POINT, SO IT IS EASILY REPLACED.

Change oil AS RECOMMENDED WHEN THE ENGINE IS WARM. THIS MOWER CAME EQUIPPED WITH AN EASY-TO-OPEN PUSH-PULL DRAIN PLUG AND PLASTIC HOSE.

Use a funnel WHEN YOU ADD NEW OIL. BE SURE NOT TO OVERFILL. CHECK THE GAUGE ON THE DIP STICK ONCE OR TWICE AS YOU FILL.

To change the oil filter, POUR SOME NEW OIL INTO A NEW FILTER AND APPLY SOME OIL ONTO THE RUBBER GASKET BEFORE INSTALLING A NEW FILTER.

To maintain a battery FOR OPTIMAL STARTING POWER, USE A WIRE BRUSH TO CLEAN THE TERMINALS.

Apply dielectric grease TO THE TERMINALS BEFORE REATTACHING THE BATTERY CABLES.

Paper air filters, HERE LOCATED BEHIND A TOOL-FREE COVER, SHOULD BE CHECKED OFTEN. TAP THE FILTER ON A HARD SURFACE TO REMOVE LOOSE DEBRIS, AND REPLACE THE FILTER WHEN THAT IS NO LONGER EFFECTIVE.

Don't use STALE GAS. DRAIN IT INTO A GAS CAN AND PUT IT IN YOUR CAR. TO DRAIN, SHUT OFF THE VALVE IN THE GAS LINE, LOOSEN THE HOSE CLAMP, AND REMOVE THE HOSE. PUT ONE END IN THE CAN, AND REOPEN THE VALVE.

Although a rear-wheel drive is generally preferred, many people like how easy it is to tip a front-wheel-drive mower onto its rear wheels to make sharp turns or reverse directions. The more complex your landscape, the more relevant this advantage may be.

Walk-Behind Mowers

Walk-behind mowers are the most ubiquitous of all yard machines. Rotary-style gasoline-engine units account for most of the market by far. Their designs have been tweaked to the point where you can usually start them with a battery and key or with a single pull of a recoil-type starter.

Mulching ability has been enhanced by improved deck and blade design. By mulching, you return nutrients to the soil and reduce the labor of bagging or raking. "Kickers" beneath the decks of Toro's Super Recycler mowers, for example, keep clippings suspended longer so they can be cut more times. Special blades with multiple edges are available as well. They cut grass into finer pieces for quicker decomposition, as well as less volume if you choose to bag.

Walk-behinds are safer than ever. The better units have a blade-brake clutch feature. When you stop to empty a collection bag or to pick up an obstacle and you let go of the bail, the blade safely stops but the engine continues to run. This eliminates the need to restart the mower, which is the case with blade-brake systems that kill the engine.

Self-Propelled versus Push

Walk-behind rotary mowers come in two basic types: self-propelled and push. There have been many innovations for the former. Ground speed controls, for example, now allow you to mow at the pace you desire. Toro's Personal Pace system conforms to your pace as you apply natural pushing pressure to the handle. You don't really have to think about it. No more need to constantly engage and disengage levers as you mow.

There are far fewer models of rotary push mowers (gasoline powered but not self-propelled), but they are still popular among budget-minded homeowners who have flat yards and don't intend to lug clippings. Push mowers are 10 to 30 pounds lighter than self-propelled mowers. They're lighter on your wallet, too—$400 versus $600 for otherwise identical units in one case. Otherwise they share many of the same features with self-propelled mowers as described above.

Electric corded and cordless units are suitable for small to average-size lawns (2,500 square feet or

Reel Mowers

Manual push reel mowers are best suited to homeowners with small lawns (under 2,000 square feet). Reel mowers cut grass like scissors instead of tearing it, as is the case with rotary mowers. According to agronomists, this is a bit better for the grass.

For the most part, manual push mowers have changed little over the years. They are lighter, weighing 16 to 32 pounds, and come in several widths, from 14 to 20 inches with four, five, or seven blades with 8- or 10-inch wheels.

Push reel mowers cut grass into fine pieces that you can let lie on the lawn (assuming you don't try to cut too much at one time), but they can be used with a collection bag. These mowers have limited height adjustability, and sharpening the blades is more difficult than sharpening most rotary blades.

less). Corded units are obviously limited to what they can mow by the location of the nearest electrical outlet and the maximum cord length, which is usually 100 feet. Their 12-amp motors produce adequate power to cut thick turf, but don't let your lawn get too tall or you'll be borrowing your neighbor's gasoline-powered mower. Some models come with a handle that flips front to back. You can mow without having to make turns at the end of each row—thereby keeping the power cord to one side of the mower and out of harm's way. Electric mowers are available in widths up to 19 inches, will mulch clippings adequately, weigh under 50 pounds, and are equipped with a safety shutoff when you release the bail. Many offer various bagging options, including side and rear.

Cordless mowers give homeowners greater range than corded mowers, but you have to remember to charge them before mowing day. The batteries will need to be replaced after five to eight years, and the blade will need regular sharpening. Otherwise these units require very little maintenance or repair. Typical run times are 30 to 45 minutes.

Buying a Self-Propelled Walk-Behind

The vast majority of self-propelled gasoline walk-behind mowers are the rotary type, meaning they

The 3-in-1 Option

BAG

MULCH

SIDE-DISCHARGE

"3-IN-1" WALK-BEHIND MOWERS OFFER THREE CUT-TING OPTIONS: BAG, MULCH, OR SIDE DISCHARGE. THE BAG OPTION, TOP, DELIVERS A MANICURED LOOK. THE MULCH OPTION, MIDDLE, MAKES SENSE FOR THOSE WHO WANT TO FEED THE LAWN BY RETURNING MULCHED CLIPPINGS TO THE LAWN. GO WITH THE SIDE-DISCHARGE OPTION, BOTTOM, TO SPREAD LARGER CLIP-PINGS ON THE LAWN. THIS TYPE OF MOWER ALLOWS THE FLEXIBILITY TO ADAPT TO CONDITIONS.

cut the grass with a horizontal blade that is attached to the vertical drive shaft of the engine. The deck is a protective housing and integral part of the mower that also supports the engine and wheels and controls the airflow to maximize the cutting and bagging efficiency. Most decks are steel, but some are aluminum alloy or high-impact plastic. Most non-commercial models (called residential or consumer models) cut a swath 21 or 22 inches wide. Most people prefer self-propelled models, even if yards are flat and small enough to be candidates for a push model.

Drive Options: Some people find it easier to maneuver a front-wheel-drive mower in a complex landscape because you can easily tilt the mower back on the rear wheels to stop or change directions. However, as long as the mower you choose has controls that enable you to easily vary ground speed and engage or disengage the drive, a rear drive is probably a better way to go. They are easier to mow a straight line and have better traction because more weight is over the rear wheels, especially when bagging.

Cutting Options: Next, consider what cutting options you want. Mulching decks and blades are designed to cut clippings so small that they quickly decompose, returning nutrients and water to the soil. Bagging clippings leaves a clean lawn, but it's more work and you must either dispose or compost the clippings. Mulching is usually the best option because most states ban the disposal of lawn waste into landfills, and because composting large quantities of grass can be problematic. Broadcasting the clippings through a side-discharge opening leaves larger clippings that dry out on the lawn and may require raking, but it's usually the best option if the lawn is overgrown.

Three-in-one models, which offer all three options, are the most versatile and by far the most popular. Two-in-one models either mulch and bag or mulch and side discharge. On most mowers, changing between modes requires no tools and is very easily and quickly accomplished. Others require a wrench or screwdriver and small parts that can get lost. Although you can buy a grass-catcher bag for a side-discharge mower, it gets in the way

Make It Easy

IT SHOULD BE EASY TO CHANGE CUTTING MODES. AVOID MODELS THAT REQUIRE TOOLS OR THAT HAVE SMALL PARTS THAT MAY GET LOST. HERE, JUST LIFT THE COVER TO INSTALL THE DISCHARGE CHUTE.

MOST REAR BAGS ARE RELATIVELY EASY TO REMOVE AND REPLACE. ON THIS MODEL, JUST LIFT THE DOOR AND LIFT THE BAG FRAME OFF (OR PLACE IT ON) THE HIGHLY VISIBLE RED SUPPORTS.

TO CHANGE FROM BAGGING TO MULCHING, A MULCH PLUG MUST FILL THE OPENING. THIS MOWER'S PLUG, INTEGRAL WITH THE DOOR, IS MORE CONVENIENT THAN MODELS WITH A SEPARATE MULCH PLUG.

and holds less. People who are buying a new mower and want to bag should only consider a rear-bagging model. If you always bag or always mulch, premium bagging or mulching blades can give better results than the multipurpose blades that typically come with the mower. On the other hand, the extra-fine clippings tend to clump more than those produced by a standard blade because the clippings are often wetter.

Wheel Sizes: Standard low-wheel models have the same size wheels on the front and rear (diameter of about 8 inches). High-wheel models, which can cost $20 to $40 more for an otherwise identical mower, have larger wheels on the rear (diameters about 9 to 12 inches) that tend to smooth the ride over bumpy turf. Wheels mounted on a full-length solid-steel axle are generally more durable than wheels that are attached to cutting height adjusters. The wheels sometimes wear out, so pay attention to the quality of the wheel, and make sure that the height-adjustment assembly is easily replaced.

Engine Options: The heart of the self-propelled mower is its engine. Noisy, two-cycle engines (those requiring that oil be mixed with gas) are a thing of the past. Today's four-cycle engines, ranging in size between 5.5 and 7 horsepower, are quieter and more efficient. All engines in this range are adequate, but the coarser the grass and the larger or hillier your lawn, the more horsepower you may need.

Overhead valve or overhead cam designs offer greater efficiency and durability and are noticeably quieter than standard side-valve engines. Many more low-priced and moderately priced mowers are available with OHV/OHC engines than in the past, and at a price that generally makes them a good value.

Makers have taken a variety of steps to make starting a self-propelled mower easier and more reliable. Some gas caps dispense fuel stabilizers to keep gas fresh. The ACRS (automatic choke recovery system) on some engines allows the user to set the choke when starting a cold engine and return to the operator's position to start the engine. The choke slowly returns to the open position as the engine warms up. Other engines need no priming or

choking. Just step up to the mower, and pull the recoil starter once or twice to start.

Convenience and comfort features are important.
For the ultimate ease, look for a key-start model.
Before you buy, try the cutting-height adjusters,
typically at each wheel, and make sure the handle-
bars are at a comfortable height and can be adjusted, especially if there will be more than one user.
Do they fold easily for compact storage? Are they
comfortable to hold? All self-propelled mowers are
equipped with a lever or bar, called a control bail,
which must be held against the handlebar for the

*Deck and blade design on "mulching"
mowers all aim to keep the cut grass
in the air so it can be cut repeatedly
by the spinning blade. Toro's Super
Recycler, for example, has "kickers"
(the angular black plastic parts on the
underside of the deck) that deflect the
cutting back down into the path of
the spinning blade.*

blade to rotate. This federally required safety feature
ensures that the blade stops when the operator
leaves the operating position (releases the bail).
Some bails are noticeably more stiff and uncomfortable to hold in place than others.

Terms You Should Know

Control Bail: A bar on all gasoline walk-behind mowers that must be held against the handle for the blade to turn, thereby ensuring that the blade will stop if the user leaves the operator position (a federal safety requirement).

Four-Cycle Engine: A small engine that, unlike a two-cycle engine, does not require the mixing of oil in the gasoline. There are a few two-cycle engine mowers out there, but most today are four-cycle.

High-Wheel Mower: Refers to walk-behind mowers with larger wheels (typically 9- to 12-inch diameter) in the rear, as compared with low-wheel mowers that have the same size wheels front and rear.

Horsepower (hp): A measure of the power of an engine. Most push mowers have between 4.0 and 6.5 hp. All are adequate for small, relatively flat lawns that push mowers typically cut.

Mulching: The process of cutting and recutting clippings into fine particles, enabling them to fall back into the turf, where they quickly decompose and restore nutrients and water to the soil.

Mulch Kit: A mulching blade and, as needed, a mulch plug, which is an insert that covers a discharge opening and maintains the circular shape on the underside of the deck when a mower is being used in the mulching mode.

OHC (overhead cam) or OHV/OHC: An OHV engine with the valves directly operated by the cam. It has fewer moving parts so it is considered to be the lightest, quietest, and most durable OHV engine design.

OHV (overhead valve): A superior engine technology that offers more power, better fuel efficiency, lower emissions, and greater durability.

Operator Presence Control (OPC): A required safety feature on all powered lawn mowers that stops the rotating blade after releasing the control bail on the handlebar of a walk-behind mower.

Recoil Starter: A starter that requires you to pull a handle attached to a rope, turning the engine to get it started. With a fresh spark plug, most engines will start with one or two pulls if you follow directions for any required priming or choking.

Side-Discharge Deflector (chute): A safety attachment used on mowers when being used in the side-discharge mode that directs clippings and debris downward and away from the operator.

Self-propelled walk-behind mowers range from single-speed to two- or three-speed to infinitely variable-speed models. Several models, including Toro's Personal Pace mower, automatically adjust speed. The more or less pressure the operator puts on the handlebar, the faster or slower the mower will move. Pull the blade control bar into the recess in the comfortable handle when you are ready to mow. This model also features a key start.

Walk-Behind Mower Maintenance Basics

Always remove the spark-plug WIRE WHEN CLEANING YOUR MOWER, CHANGING BLADES, OR WORKING ON THE ENGINE.

Use a spark-plug SOCKET WRENCH TO REMOVE A SPARK PLUG FOR INSPECTION OR REPLACEMENT. USE A REPLACEMENT THAT IS PREGAPPED FOR YOUR ENGINE.

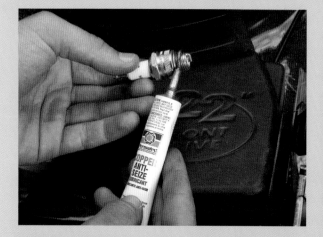

Apply copper anti-seize lubricant TO THE SPARK PLUG'S THREADS TO MAKE FUTURE REMOVAL EASIER.

Keep your engine's COOLING FINS FREE OF DEBRIS. USE A SMALL DOWEL FOR THE CHORE.

Tap a dirty air filter ON A HARD SURFACE TO REMOVE LOOSE DEBRIS, AND USE AN OLD PAINT BRUSH TO REMOVE LOOSE DIRT.

Replace it WHEN THAT IS NO LONGER EFFECTIVE. WIPE DIRT OUT OF THE HOUSING AND ITS COVER BEFORE YOU REINSTALL A CLEANED AIR FILTER OR INSTALL A NEW FILTER.

When tilting THE MOWER TO ACCESS THE UNDERSIDE FOR MAINTENANCE, PREVENT GAS LEAKAGE BY PLACING A PLASTIC BAG OVER THE OPENING UNDER THE CAP.

To remove (OR REINSTALL) A BLADE, INSERT A WOOD BLOCK TO KEEP THE BLADE FROM TURNING AS YOU APPLY PRESSURE ON THE LOCKING BOLT.

If sharpening YOUR OWN BLADE, USE A FILE TO RE-MOVE EQUAL AMOUNTS OF MATERIAL FROM EACH SIDE, AND CHECK THE BALANCE AS SHOWN.

Reinstall A NEW BLADE USING A TORQUE WRENCH TO THE TORQUE SPECIFIED IN YOUR MANUAL.

Use a putty knife TO REMOVE CAKED-ON CLIPPINGS FROM THE UNDERSIDE OF YOUR MOWER DECK. DOING SO WILL IMPROVE BAGGING AND MULCHING EFFICIENCY.

Don't use STALE GAS (GAS MORE THAN THREE WEEKS OLD). INSTEAD, DRAIN YOUR TANK INTO A GAS CAN USING A SIPHON, AND POUR IT IN YOUR CAR'S GAS TANK.

What You'll Need for Lawn Care

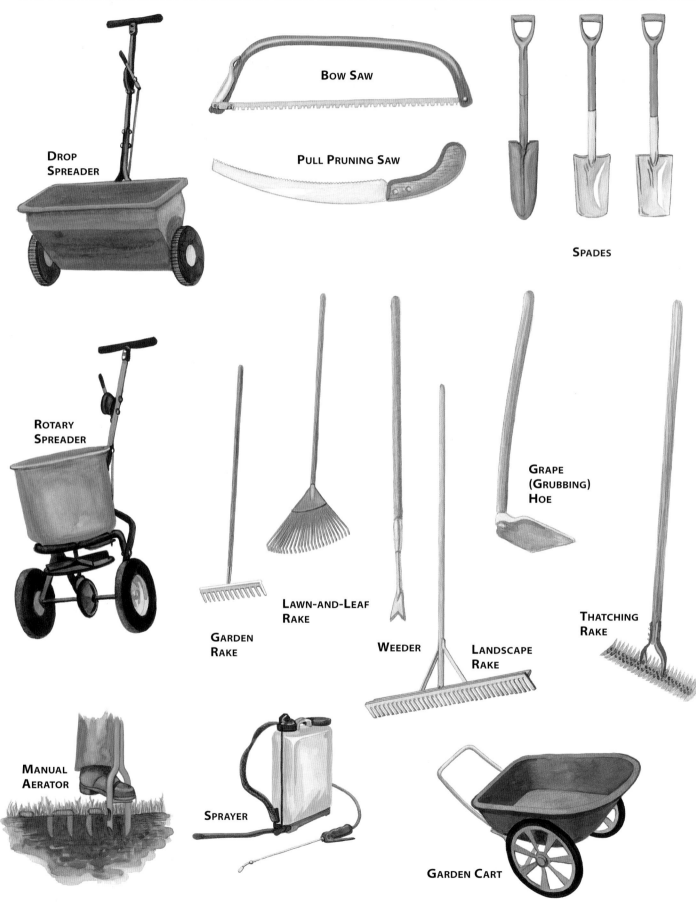

DROP SPREADER

BOW SAW

PULL PRUNING SAW

SPADES

ROTARY SPREADER

GARDEN RAKE

LAWN-AND-LEAF RAKE

WEEDER

LANDSCAPE RAKE

GRAPE (GRUBBING) HOE

THATCHING RAKE

MANUAL AERATOR

SPRAYER

GARDEN CART

D-Handled Shovel

Long-Handled Shovel

Turf Edger

Pruning Shears

Loppers

Grass Shears

Other Lawn Tools

Lawn tools fall into three categories: tools you should own, tools helpful to own if you have the budget and space, and tools used so seldom they are best rented. The following recommendations assume average situations. Your needs may differ.

Tools to Own

The tools and machines in this group are essential to a good lawn-care program.

Spreader Precision of application is the main difference between the two types of spreaders. A drop spreader distributes seed, fertilizer, and other amendments, such as lime, in swaths the width of the spreader. Settings allow you to control the amount distributed. A rotary spreader flings seed or amendments over a wide area, thereby covering ground faster than drop spreaders. However, it is not well suited for use on windy days or with small, irregularly shaped lawns.

Sprayer You will need a sprayer for dispensing insecticidal soap or oil solutions. Sprayers are typically available in canister or backpack styles with 2- to 4-gallon polyethylene tanks and interchangeable nozzles for varying application patterns and rates.

Spade Often mistakenly called a shovel, spades have flat or gently curved blades and are used for planting or transplanting, edging, and turf removal.

Round-point shovel These are designed to move large quantities of fine-textured material, such as sand, soil, or nonfibrous mulches, from one place to another.

Garden rake The steel-headed type is useful for preparing small areas of soil for the planting of seed, plugs, or sprigs.

Lawn-and-leaf rake Lawn rakes are useful for collecting lightweight material, such as clippings and leaves. Those made from bamboo are usually the lightest and easiest to use. Typically, however, they last only a few seasons before falling apart. Steel rakes and the modern plastics are more durable.

Landscape rake This has a wide, 36-inch aluminum head mounted on an aluminum or wood shaft. Use it to remove debris from prepared soil and to level the soil prior to planting a new lawn.

Thatching rake The thatching rake is designed to remove thatch from your lawn without damaging the turf. The angle of the rake head can be adjusted to control the depth of the tine penetration.

Pruning tools Use pruning shears for branches up to ½ inch, lopping shears for ½- to 1½-inch branches, pruning saws for woody branches up to 3 inches in diameter, and a bow saw for larger branches.

Manual aerator Foot-powered and easy to use, a manual aerator is fine if you have a small lawn and time on your hands.

Grape (grubbing) hoe This wide, heavy-bladed hoe offers a low-tech but efficient way to remove turf you no longer want.

Grass shears Shears provide a time-honored but slow means of clipping grass along the edge of a garden bed. Clipping with shears is valuable where your prized flowers grow too close to the path of an indiscriminate string trimmer.

Weeder The forked steel head on a short, hardwood handle allows the prying of weeds from turf.

Turf edger A half-moon-shaped steel cutting head is mounted to a hardwood handle. Use it to keep lawn edges neat or to trim away excess when laying sod along irregular lawn edges.

Garden cart or wheelbarrow These indispensable aids haul everything from lawn tools and fertilizer to weeds and prunings.

Specialty Tools

The following tools are convenient to own if your budget and storage space allow.

Power edger This is a gasoline- or electric-powered tool with a short blade that you can use horizontally to trim grass at lawn edges or vertically to create and maintain edges.

String trimmer There are gas-, electric-, and battery-powered models. A plastic line at the cutting end rotates at a high speed to trim grass or weeds along lawn edges and near fixtures, such as lampposts and fences. The better-balanced and easier-to-use models have the power unit at the top end of a long shaft and an adjustable handle in the middle. Cutting swaths range from 6 to 10 inches for cordless units, 8 to 15 inches for corded electric models, and 15 to 18 inches for gas-powered units.

Pole trimmer This is a pruning saw at the end of a 12-foot telescoping pole. It's great for homeowners who like to do high pruning with their feet firmly planted on the ground.

Blowers Powered by gas or electricity, these machines blow leaves into piles for easier collection. Blowers are available in either hand-held, wheeled, or backpack styles, with the last two types leaving you less tired on big jobs. Even if you like raking leaves on the lawn, you'll appreciate a blower's help in moving leaves out from under shrubs. Many units can be converted to vacuums and are useful for cleaning up and mulching small quantities of leaves. Electric blowers produce less noise than gas-powered units and have no emissions.

■ *Buy As You Go*

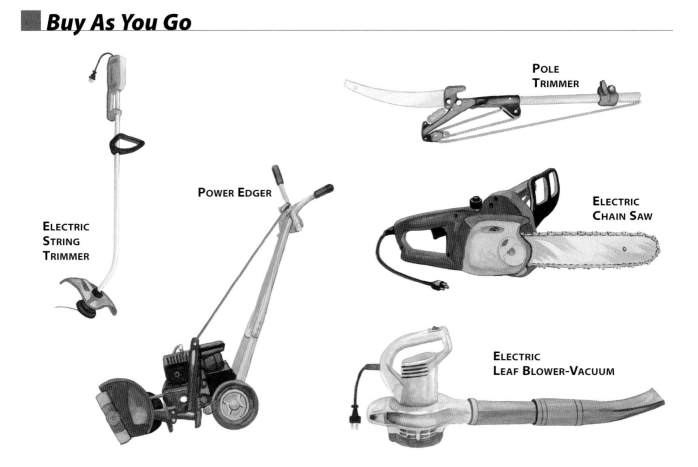

ELECTRIC STRING TRIMMER

POWER EDGER

POLE TRIMMER

ELECTRIC CHAIN SAW

ELECTRIC LEAF BLOWER-VACUUM

Chain saw For the cutting of small tree limbs and trunks in an average-size yard, an electric saw can be a smarter buy than a gas-powered saw. If you can keep all your cutting within 100 feet or so of an outdoor electrical outlet, it will handle most chores, even cutting firewood. In contrast to bigger, heavier gas-powered chain saws, electric saws emit no exhaust fumes and are low maintenance, low cost, quiet, and always ready to go.

Tools to Rent

Some of the tools in this group are expensive; others take up a lot of space and aren't needed often.

Power aerator Available in several styles, aerators loosen compacted soil by making many small holes in it. The best units have hollow coring devices that lift plugs of soil and turf from the lawn as the unit passes over it. Less-effective units create holes by pushing spikes into the lawn.

Power tiller These are available in many styles and capacities, from small soil mixers to large, 8-horsepower units. Tillers are ideal for alleviating compaction in preparation for a new lawn or for mixing in soil amendments, such as lime, fertilizer, and compost. Some tillers are available with power rake and aerating attachments.

Lawn roller Use this tool to prepare soil for planting. While inexpensive, it does take up storage space, so you may want to rent when you need one.

Power dethatcher This gas-powered tool (not shown) has heavy, metal tines that whip the lawn as you pass the machine over it. Power rakes are great for removing light thatch and for prepping a lawn for overseeding.

Vertical mower Resembling a lawn mower, a vertical mower (not shown) is useful for dethatching and for scarifying the soil in preparation for seeding. This mower has several vertically mounted blades that are set to slightly penetrate the soil.

Power seeder (slit seeder) Similar to the vertical mower, this gasoline-powered unit (not shown) cuts many shallow grooves in prepared soil or turf and sows grass seed into them at recommended rates.

■ *Tools to Rent*

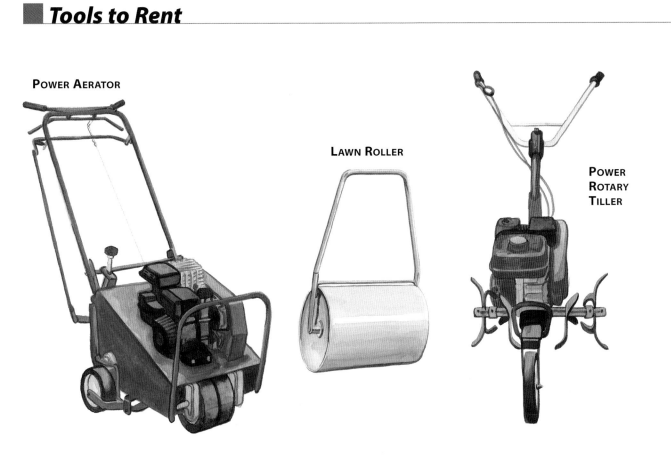

POWER AERATOR

LAWN ROLLER

POWER ROTARY TILLER

Reducing Lawn Maintenance

There are plenty of things you can do to reduce the time and money spent on maintaining your lawn. We've already discussed the machines that can help you get the job done faster. In this chapter, we'll focus on low-tech ways to prevent your grass from growing too fast. You can make a big difference by doing small things, such as cutting your lawn at the appropriate height and using slow-release fertilizers. You can also realize big savings by changing your attitude about what constitutes a beautiful lawn. Clover, for example, is not an undesirable. A sprinkling of violets is quite beautiful. Midsummer periods when your grass temporarily turns brown is simply natural. Just remember: early lawns were inspired by grassy openings in the forest, not by golf courses or pictures in magazines.

Eliminate one of five annual mowings by keeping your blade set high. The right height for you depends on your grass type.

Set the Right Height

There are several reasons not to cut your grass too short. First, grass grows from the crown, not the blade tips. This trait makes grass ideal for lawns because it keeps on growing despite the regular mowing off of its upper stem, leaf sheath, and blades. This is also why it's important not to damage grass crowns by accidental scalping with the mower. No crown, no grass! Second, keeping grass on the longer side allows it greater surface area to carry out photosynthesis. This in turn results in healthier plants. Third, taller grass grows slower than shorter grass. You can use this simple fact to eliminate up to 20 percent of the mowing you do annually. That's a savings of about eight hours a year for the average lawn owner, not to mention the savings of gasoline and wear on equipment. Lastly, by keeping your grass at the upper

Timesavers

IT'S EASIER TO ADJUST CUTTING HEIGHT IF YOU SUPPORT ONE SIDE OF THE MOWER AT A TIME ON A WOOD BLOCK TO GET THE WEIGHT OFF THE WHEELS THAT YOU ARE TRYING TO ADJUST.

MAKE YOUR NEW MOWER'S DECK EASIER TO CLEAN BY SPRAYING COOKING SPRAY ON THE UNDERSIDE OF THE DECK.

IF YOU USE YOUR MOWER INFREQUENTLY, OR ARE STORING IT AWAY FOR THE OFF-SEASON, FILL THE TANK WITH FUEL THAT HAS BEEN TREATED WITH A FUEL STABILIZER.

Recommended Mowing Heights

Grass Type	Inches
Annual ryegrass	2 to 2½
Bahiagrass	2 to 3
Bermudagrass	1 to 1½
Centipedegrass	1½ to 2
Fine fescue	2 to 2½
Kentucky bluegrass	2½ to 3
Perennial ryegrass	2 to 2½
St. Augustinegrass	2 to 3
Tall fescue	2½ to 3½
Zoysiagrass	1 to 2

end of its recommended mowing height, you can prevent most weeds from germinating—and thereby eliminate the need for herbicides.

When to Mow

Most cool-season grasses should be cut when they reach heights of 3 to 3½ inches—typically once a week. Warm-season grasses should be cut when they reach 2 to 2½ inches. Cut no more than one-third of the grass height at each mowing to avoid damaging the plants. If the lawn grows too high for you to cut off one-third of the height and have an acceptable length, cut off one-third now and mow one-third off again in two or three days. Cutting more than one-third the height results in clumps of clippings that tend to lie on top of the lawn, decompose more slowly, and give the grass a less attractive, open, bristly appearance. If this does happen, however, you can always take the rake, make a pile, and move it to the compost bin when you're done or take the leaf blower and blow the clumps to smithereens. But it is far easier to cut the lawn when it needs it and reduce the extra work. In addition, short cutting will stunt or slow root grow and weaken the grass plants.

Rules for Smart Mowing

BY SETTING CUTTING HEIGHTS CORRECTLY, YOU CAN GREATLY REDUCE WEED GROWTH AND MOWING FREQUENCY.

YOU CAN EASILY SEE THE DIFFERENCE BETWEEN GRASS THAT WAS CUT WITH DULL (LEFT) AND SHARP BLADES.

- *Cut no more than one-third the height of the grass in any single mowing.*
- *Never scalp the lawn or cut below plant crowns.*
- *Mow only when the grass is dry.*
- *Mow with a sharp blade. Resharpen after every 10 hours of mowing. Bring the blade to a professional sharpening service once a year. Replace the blade as necessary.*
- *Change mowing patterns frequently to prevent soil compaction.*
- *Leave clippings on the lawn unless they are very long or wet.*
- *Rinse clippings off your mower after it has cooled to reduce the chance of spreading lawn disease.*
- *Cut grass at the high end of the recommended height range during hot weather.*
- *Cut at the low end of the recommended height range during cool weather or in shade.*
- *Make your last cut of the season at the low end of the recommended height range.*

Don't Bother with Bagging

Leave clippings where they fall. This will not only save you the labor of collecting and composting them but will also reduce the need for adding fertilizer because the clippings add nitrogen to the soil as they decompose. Clippings also act as a light mulch that helps to conserve soil moisture. However, if you have neglected your mowing or must mow in wet conditions, the long clippings are likely to form heavy clumps that cover the grass. In such cases, remove the clippings so that they do not smother the grass plants beneath them.

The idea of leaving clippings on the lawn is not new, but today's mulching mowers, also called recycling mowers, make it even easier to leave clippings where they fall. The deck and blade designs allow these mowers to cut each grass blade several times, producing a finely chopped clipping.

Avoid Overwatering

Try to give your lawn the water it needs—and no more. This moderate approach conserves an important resource, saves money, and helps prevent grass diseases caused by too much water. How much water your lawn needs depends on the type of grass in the turf, the overall health of your lawn and soil,

Conservation Measures

CUT SEVERAL CORE SAMPLES, MEASURE, AND AVERAGE THE ROOT LENGTHS. THEN REPLACE THE SAMPLES.

USE A RAIN GAUGE TO MONITOR RAINFALL. DON'T WATER IF NATURE HAS DONE THE JOB FOR YOU.

IF YOU'RE USING PORTABLE SPRINKLERS, MECHANICAL TIMERS CAN HELP YOU IRRIGATE MORE EFFICIENTLY.

the amount of rainfall your lawn gets, and the climate. You may need as few as two waterings a year or as many as two a week.

The best approach to watering grass (and most other plants) is to follow nature's pattern of rainy periods followed by brief dry spells. Apply enough water all at once to penetrate the roots, let the soil almost dry out, and apply water again. Grass signals that it needs water by losing its spring: when you walk across the lawn and see your footprints, your lawn probably needs to be watered.

To determine how much water your lawn needs, you need to consider several factors: the depth of its roots, soil type and its "penetrability," your irrigation method, and, of course, the weather. First, check to see how deep the roots of your grass are. To do this, use a shovel to remove several samples from around the yard. Average the root lengths, and add an inch to the average root depth to arrive at a target watering depth. It makes no sense to waste water by watering to a level substantially deeper than your lawn's root zone.

Root depth depends on how much time you have taken to improve your soil and on the type of grass you are growing. Some grasses, such as tall fescues, have roots that reach 1 foot deep. Others grow to only half that, in even the best conditions. As your grass develops deeper roots, adjust your watering-depth target so that you continue to encourage roots to go deeper.

Next, determine how much water is needed to moisten soil to your target root zone. Wait for a four- to five-day dry spell, and then set out some empty cans (6-ounce tuna cans work well) in various locations on the lawn. Run your sprinkler or in-ground sprinkler system until the cans contain 1 inch of water. Record the amount of time it takes. Then wait a day to allow the water to penetrate the soil, and check the depth it has reached. If 1 inch of water moistens soil to a depth beyond the root depth, try the procedure again after your soil has dried, but turn off the sprinklers sooner. Conversely, if the root depth is not reached, try running your sprinklers longer. Base future waterings on what you have learned from your observations. If it rains during the week, decrease your watering by the amount of rain that fell. If it's hot and sunny or windy, you may need to increase the watering amount and frequency.

A good rule of thumb for most grasses is 1 to 2 inches per week. If you have porous soil that drains quickly, you would apply 1 inch of water twice a week. Conversely, if your soil holds water well, a good guess would be 1½ to 2 inches once a week.

Fertilizer Basics

Grasses require at least 16 different essential elements in their diets, most of which are available from the plants' surrounding environment. But the extraordinary growth demands of today's lawn owners usually mean that homeowners must help Mother Nature along.

Even if you are committed to having a low-maintenance lawn, you will need to fertilize it with nitrogen (N) to sustain thick, vigorous turf. In addition to bringing on deep green color, nitrogen is responsible for the sturdy growth and shoot density needed to fight off weeds and to stand up to diseases, insects, and traffic.

All these positive effects can easily turn into negatives if you use too much fertilizer or apply it at the wrong time. The common practice of fertilizing in early spring is actually not the best time in northern climates. It not only encourages excess blade growth, which means more mowing, but it also gives your weeds a boost and increases thatch! Excessive spring growth also produces thin-walled grass blade cells that are more prone to injury, disease, and insects. Late summer to early fall is the preferred time for feeding northern lawns; mid-spring in the South.

In addition to needing nitrogen, your lawn may need phosphorus (P) and potassium (K). Depending on where you live, your soil may naturally contain adequate levels of these elements. Aiding in root growth and improving establishment rates, phosphorus is needed in small amounts and tends to remain in the soil. Potassium plays an important role in enhancing your grass's resistance to cold, disease, drought, and wear, and is more prone to leaching from the soil. A soil test will help you determine which nutrients your soil needs. (See

Smarter Fertilizing

FERTILIZER RATIOS AND GRADES TELL CONSUMERS HOW MANY POUNDS OF NUTRIENTS ARE CONTAINED IN 100 LBS. OF THE PRODUCT. FERTILIZER RATIOS INDICATE THE RELATIVE AMOUNTS OF NITROGEN (N), PHOSPHORUS (P), AND POTASSIUM (K).

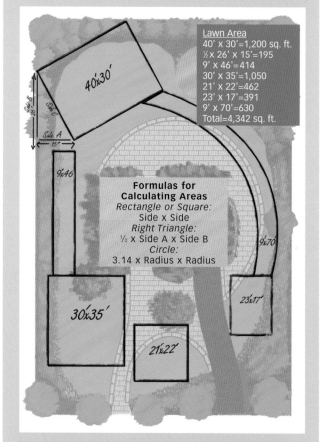

TO FIGURE OUT HOW MUCH FERTILIZER (OR ANY OTHER SOIL AMENDMENTS) TO BUY, DIVIDE YOUR LAWN INTO SIMPLE GEOGRAPHIC SHAPES, AND THEN CALCULATE THE AREAS OF THE SHAPES USING THE FORMULAS ABOVE.

Slow-Release versus Fast-Release Fertilizers

	ADVANTAGES	DISADVANTAGES
SLOW RELEASE	• Nitrogen released gradually • Less apt to leach • Low incidence of burning • Fewer applications used • Lasts longer	• Higher initial cost • Dependent on warm weather for release • Takes longer for turfgrass response
FAST RELEASE	• Immediate nitrogen availability • Generally costs less • Better-known release rate • Releases even in cold weather	• More apt to leach, especially on sandy soils • More apt to burn foliage • May raise salinity of soil • More frequent applications required • May acidify soil and make it less hospitable to beneficial microorganisms • May thin cell walls and make plants vulnerable to disease • Requires more frequent watering

Nitrogen Fertilizers

As discussed in the text, the fertilizers listed below are commonly available at nurseries and garden centers.

Fast-Release Nitrogen Fertilizers

• Ammonium nitrate
• Ammonium phosphate
• Ammonium sulfate
• Calcium nitrate
• Urea

Slow-Release Nitrogen Fertilizers

• Activated sludge
• Alfalfa meal
• Bone meal
• Composted manure
• Dried poultry waste
• IBDU (isobutylidene diurea)
• Methylene urea
• Soybean meal
• Sulfur-coated urea
• Ureaformaldehyde

"Getting a Soil Test," page 45.)

A fertilizer with the designation "complete" contains all three of these nutritional elements. The percentage of the bag's contents made up respectively of nitrogen, phosphorus, and potassium can be found by looking at the fertilizer grade. These three prominent numbers also tell you the percentage of nitrogen to phosphorus to potassium. For example, in a 50-pound bag of 20-10-10 grade, the ratio is 2:1:1, which means that 20 percent of the 50 pounds, or 10 pounds of the bag, is actual nitrogen; 10 percent (5 pounds) is phosphorus; and 10 percent (5 pounds) is potassium. The remaining 30 pounds of material in the bag may consist of additional elements such as iron and sulfur, as well as inert "filler" ingredients. Fillers are used to help ensure even distribution of the product and are frequently made from organic materials such as finely ground corn cobs.

Ratios are helpful in choosing which fertilizer to use for specific purposes. Those with a 1:2:2 ratio, such as 6-12-12 fertilizer, are lower in nitrogen but higher in the nutrients desired when planting new grass or renovating old lawns. Fertilizers with high-nitrogen ratios of 2:1:1, 4:1:2, or 3:1:2 are frequently used for maintenance applications. They contain N, P, and K quantities closer to the plant's ongoing needs and are available in grades of 12-6-6, 16-8-8, 20-10-10, 12-4-8, and so on.

In considering which bag of fertilizer is most appropriate for your yard, be sure to read the back label for the guaranteed analysis of the contents.

If your soil test indicates that you don't need to add phosphorus or potassium, choose a bag with a low numeral or zero for that element. For example, a bag of 20-0-5 would have no phosphorus.

In addition to checking the grade, you should also determine what type of nitrogen has been used, water-soluble or water-insoluble. Water-soluble nitrogen, once watered into the soil, can be immediately used by grass plants. Ammonium nitrate, ammonium sulfate, and urea are examples of this quick-release form of nitrogen. They provide a rapid green-up but also have drawbacks, as shown in the table "Slow-Release versus Fast-Release Fertilizers" on page 117. Water-insoluble nitrogen, found in slow-release fertilizers, must first be broken down by soil microbes into forms grass plants can use. These slow-release sources include synthetic organics, such as ureaforms, or those derived from natural organic materials, such as composted manures.

To spread the release of nitrogen over time, fertilizer companies can also manipulate the size of particles and sometimes coat them as well. Because these forms take longer to dissolve, they release nitrogen at varying rates. Common examples are isobutylidene diurea (IBDU) and sulfur-coated ureas.

When buying fertilizer, opt for the water-insoluble types or other slow-release forms. Using slow-release fertilizers will allow you to reduce the amount of time you spend behind your spreader. They last much longer and don't have to be applied as frequently as fast-release fertilizers, saving you money as well as time. Determine the type of fertilizer you have by reading the guaranteed analysis on the bag. Note: many fertilizers have a combination of both fast-release and slow-release types of nitrogen. You should check carefully to find products that derive a majority of their nitrogen from slow-release sources,

Fertilizer Guidelines

- *Test soil to determine grade and amount of fertilizer to use.*
- *Apply no more than 1 pound of fast-release nitrogen per 1,000 square feet in a single application.*
- *Cool-season lawns should receive most of their yearly fertilizer in the early fall.*
- *Fertilize warm-season lawns from early spring until late summer.*
- *Use slow-release nitrogen whenever possible, especially on sandy soils.*
- *Wait until warm-season grass becomes dormant before fertilizing areas overseeded for winter color.*
- *Use only the amount called for, based on your lawn's square footage.*
- *For quicker application and to avoid a striped fertilizer pattern in the grass, use a rotary spreader, which applies fertilizer more evenly.*
- *Spread the fertilizer in two directions for each application.*
- *Apply fertilizer to dry grass, and water well immediately afterward.*
- *Sweep up any fertilizer spilled on paved areas and save for later use.*
- *Don't use leftover lawn fertilizer on trees, shrubs, annuals, or perennials. Too much nitrogen on these plants stimulates stem and leaf growth, decreases flower and fruit production, and sends an open invitation to chewing and sucking insects that feed on the nitrogen-rich foliage.*

such as soybean meal or composted manure.

How Much and When?

The optimal time to apply fertilizers is when the grass roots and blades are actively growing. In the North this growth season occurs during the early to mid fall, when weed competition is minimal and fertilizing produces healthy root growth. This timing also allows plants to build up needed carbohydrate stores with just a moderate amount of top-growth. For northern lawns, you should divide the annual amount of fertilizer and apply two-thirds in early fall and the remainder in mid to late spring, after the lawn's initial green-up. Because the grasses in southern lawns have a larger blade size and grow more vigorously, they will need at least two applications of fertilizer each year. Do the first about three weeks after the initial spring green-up; then fertilize again in late summer. You can add supplemental quick-release nitrogen between these times if weak growth and poor color indicate that it's needed.

For low-maintenance lawns, you should be applying 2 pounds of nitrogen per 1,000 square feet per year in the North and 2 to 4 pounds in the South. This may require an adjustment, given your specific growing environment, soil test results, the lawn's condition, and the type of fertilizer you use,

What's Organic Fertilizer?

In the fertilizer industry, the term *organic* is used to refer to any product containing carbon in its chemical structure. This means that man-made forms such as ureaformaldehyde are called organic along with "natural" fertilizers, such as composted manure. While both kinds of materials supply slow-release nitrogen to your grass, natural, or nonsynthetic, fertilizers do more than just add nutrients to the soil. They improve the overall condition of the soil and increase the number of beneficial microorganisms residing in it. Unfortunately, natural fertilizers would need to be spread in large quantities to meet lawn fertilization requirements. So, the best strategy is to use natural fertilizers to supplement a yearly dose of synthetic fertilizer.

Prevent Thatch Buildup

The best way to control thatch is to avoid a buildup in the first place. Here are some maintenance practices that will help.
• Cut grass at the recommended height for your turf at regular intervals to avoid depositing too many clippings on the lawn at one time.
• Fertilize only in the fall to reduce excessive growth. Promote microbial life by maintaining a proper soil pH.
• Aerate your lawn once a year. If thatch does begin to accumulate to undesirable levels, apply a topdressing of a compost-and-soil mixture prior to aerating in the spring and fall. The organic matter will promote microbial activity, which will help decompose thatch.

whether slow- or fast-release. You can consult your Cooperative Extension Service for local recommendations. Fast-release fertilizers are usually applied at a rate of 1 pound of nitrogen per 1,000 square feet. Slow-release fertilizers usually require a higher rate of application to deliver their nitrogen. Follow the manufacturer's instructions and check the calibration of your spreader, as well as the square footage of your lawn, to ensure that you are applying the right amount. Remember, more is not necessarily better with fertilizers. Applying too much may "burn" your lawn and promote thatch formation, disease, and insect infestation.

Keep in mind that well-watered lawns or those subject to heavy rainfall will require more nitrogen than their unwatered counterparts. Sandy soils are more prone to leach nutrients, but using water-insoluble fertilizers will help nutrients remain in the soil longer. Leaving grass clippings on the lawn over the course of a year will add about 1 pound of nitrogen per 1,000 square feet, so you can figure accordingly. The total amount of nitrogen that you'll need per year also varies with the type of grass you are growing. For example, Kentucky bluegrass and perennial ryegrasses require more fertilizer than the fescues, while in the South, Bermudagrass, zoysiagrass, and St. Augustinegrass need more than bahiagrass, centipedegrass, or carpetgrass.

Lawn Irrigation Systems

If you plan on maintaining a sizable lawn and want to keep it green during the growing season, a permanent in-ground irrigation system can conserve water and save time, too. A properly installed system can deliver just the right amount of water when and where your lawn needs it, and it eliminates the need to drag portable sprinklers and hoses all over the yard. In-ground sprinkler systems also make sense for a vacation home that you visit irregularly or if you travel frequently and are not always home in the summer to attend to your lawn's water needs. Rain sensors and other weather-monitoring equipment help prevent your system from coming on when the lawn doesn't need watering.

Sprinkler heads come in several varieties. This rotary model pops up out of its housing when water pressure is introduced and can deliver water in a 20- to 360-deg. arc.

How Sprinkler Systems Work

A typical in-ground sprinkler system delivers water via a network of underground pipes to all areas of a lawn. It consists of multiple control valves, each of which can either stop or start the flow of water to an area of lawn, or zone. Each zone consists of several sprinkler heads attached to buried pipes by risers (short vertical pipes) that are arranged to provide uniform water coverage to the grass in that area. Systems are divided into zones because household water pressure is capable of supplying only a limited number of sprinklers at one time.

There are two types of in-ground sprinkler systems: manual and automatic. A fully automated in-ground system will typically include a programmable controller that allows you to schedule when and where various portions of your lawn will be watered. A signal from the controller activates a solenoid, also called an electromechanical valve, that opens or closes at the programmed times.

System Basics

ROTARY SPRINKLER HEADS WATER LARGE AREAS IN SWEEPING ARCS. THE MOVEMENT IS POWERED BY WATER PRESSURE AND DRIVEN WITH GEARS.

SPRAY-TYPE SPRINKLER HEADS DO NOT ROTATE. THEY SPRAY WATER IN VARIOUS PATTERNS AND ARE BETTER SUITED TO SMALLER AREAS.

WHEN WATER PRESSURE IS OFF, SPRINKLER HEADS RETRACT BELOW MOWING HEIGHTS.

SOME SPRAY HEADS CAN BE SITE ADJUSTED TO ENSURE EVEN COVERAGE. THIS MODEL ALLOWS YOU TO SET THE SPRAY TRAJECTORY ANYWHERE FROM **7** TO **25** DEG.

IN LAWN AREAS USED FOR RECREATIONAL PURPOSES, SUCH AS BACKYARD GAMES AND SPORTS, SPRINKLER HEADS CAN BE LOCATED IN GARDEN BEDS.

Some automatic systems are equipped with moisture sensors (weather or soil) that override the controller program and prevent the system from turning on during rainy weather or after rain while the soil remains moist. A manual system requires that you turn the control valves on and off by hand.

There are several types of sprinkler heads, including sprayers that deliver a fine, mist-like spray and rotary heads that throw water in a wide circle, much like a portable rotary sprinkler does. Spray-type heads are specified for systems when accuracy of coverage is critical. Rotary heads deliver water to larger areas, so fewer are required. Pop-up varieties of each type of sprinkler head, spray and rotary, rise several inches above grade level when water pressure is introduced. This ensures that ground covers and low shrubs don't interfere with water delivery.

Sprinkler heads are installed in either triangular or square grid layouts. Make sure that the spray from one sprinkler head reaches the next one, for head-to-head coverage. For example, if you install sprinkler heads with a 12-foot radius, place sprinklers no more than 12 feet apart. Many sprinkler heads can be adjusted to control the amount of water delivered. They can also be adjusted to deliver water in a variety of patterns. A full head delivers water in a full circular pattern. The other circular patterns are half, quarter, and adjustable. Adjustable spray heads can water any part of a circle, from 0 to about 360 degrees. Rotary heads adjust from 20 to

Start with a Plan

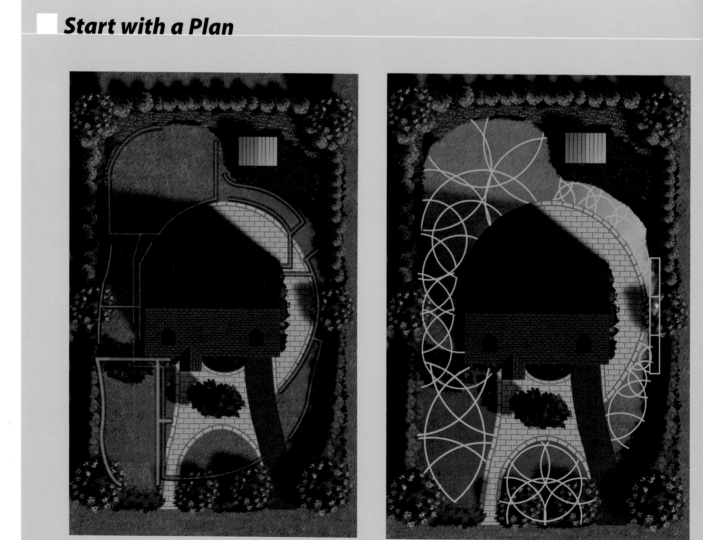

360 degrees. There are also rectangular and square patterns for narrow rectangles of turf or perfectly square areas, and there are end-strip, center-strip, and side-strip patterns for grassy pathways, side yards, and other tight spaces.

Assessing Your System

A well-designed sprinkler system will deliver water evenly to all grass areas. It's important to select heads that provide the right spray pattern for your needs but that also avoid overspray onto driveways, streets, paths, patios, buildings, and unwary passersby. Also, avoid placing a sprinkler where it will spray directly onto the trunks of trees and thereby damage the bark. The sheer force of the

Far left THE COLOR LINES ON THE PLAN SHOW THE IRRIGATION SYSTEM'S PIPE LAYOUT. EACH ZONE IS REPRESENTED BY A DIFFERENT COLOR.

Left THE ARCS INDICATE THE DIFFERENT PATTERNS OF THE SPRAY HEADS USED TO MAKE AN EFFICIENT, FULL-COVERAGE SYSTEM.

Below SPRAY HEADS—THE DEVICES THAT DELIVER WATER TO YOUR LAWN—ARE AVAILABLE WITH NUMEROUS SPRAY PATTERNS THAT FIT NEARLY EVERY CONCEIVABLE LANDSCAPE SITUATION, FROM NARROW AND IRREGULARLY SHAPED TURF AREAS TO LARGE EXPANSES OF OPEN LAWN. CHOOSE THE PATTERNS THAT MINIMIZE OVERSPRAY ONTO SIDEWALKS, DRIVEWAYS, OR OTHER PLANTING AREAS: 1 FULL; 2 HALF; 3 QUARTER; 4 SIDE STRIP; 5 CENTER STRIP; 6 SQUARE; 7 ADJUSTABLE; 8 END STRIP.

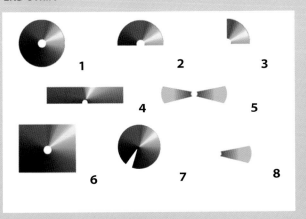

water pressure can score the bark, and constant wetting weakens it, making it more susceptible to pests and diseases. Misdirected spray can also blast the petals off of flowers. The plan shown on the preceding page is designed for maximum turf irrigation efficiency, but it could be altered to water the planting beds as well. If you suspect uneven coverage—several parts of your lawn tend to be dry and brown, for example—try a simple test to be sure your sprinkler system is to blame. Place six containers, such as tuna cans, throughout the affected area, and run your system. Note the depth of water collected in each can, and calculate an average depth. Perform the same test in areas that seem to receive adequate water (preferably at the same time of day to avoid variations due to fluctuations in water pressure), and make your comparison. If one area is receiving ¾ inch of water in an hour and another is getting only ¼ inch, make adjustments. If necessary, redesign your system using newer technology sprinklers that deliver even coverage. Otherwise you will have to choose between two evils: continuing to deliver inadequate water to some areas and risking brown patches, or using more water than necessary elsewhere to ensure adequate coverage to areas with an inadequate rate of delivery.

Most of the materials for an in-ground sprinkler system require only a hacksaw or pipe cutter and glue for assembly. Get professional help, however, with designing a plan.

Improve Efficiency

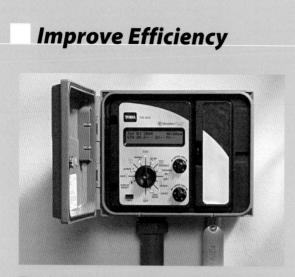

TORO'S INTELLI-SENSE ET CONTROLLER RECEIVES DATA FROM WEATHER STATIONS AND RECALCULATES WATERING TIMES DAILY.

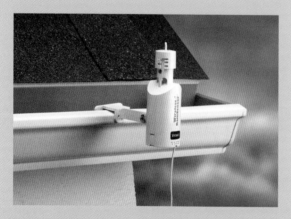

RAIN SENSORS, SUCH AS THE MODEL SHOWN, WILL SHUT DOWN AN IRRIGATION SYSTEM AFTER IT BEGINS TO RAIN, CONSERVING WATER.

AUTOMATIC CONTROL VALVES WILL GENERALLY SAVE WATER AND PRODUCE A HEALTHIER LAWN. MANUAL VALVES CAN BE RETROFITTED WITH AUTOMATED VALVES TO SAVE WATER.

Installing an In-Ground Sprinkler

If you decide to install an in-ground irrigation system yourself, you won't need to be completely on your own. The major manufacturers offer free assistance to homeowners who want to design and install their own systems. One option is to have the manufacturer design your system, and then install it yourself. Some manufacturers design the system free of charge and provide installation instructions and a shopping list of all the parts you'll need. Many companies also offer free advice over the phone or online, such as torodesign.com. However, the easiest alternative is to hire a contractor to do the installation for you. Irrigation contractors own the right tools, know local codes and regulations, and can sometimes complete the whole job in an afternoon after an initial site evaluation.

Lawn Irrigation Gets Smarter

Water costs are rising and legislation to prevent wastage, especially in regions where water is scarce, is increasing, too. Sprinkler system manufacturers are meeting these challenges with a new, efficient generation of irrigation system controllers that conserve water. Controllers are the "brains" of automated sprinkler systems. They tell the automatic valves that control each sprinkler zone in your yard when to open and close based on the watering program that's been entered into the controller. The new controllers utilize weather data and site conditions to determine the ET, or evapotranspiration. ET refers to water loss from evaporation (from soil) and transpiration (from plants). The controllers use this

DOING IT YOURSELF?

Smart TIP

If you choose to tackle the installation yourself, check with local building officials. Codes may require specific backflow or anti-siphon devices, which prevent irrigation-system water from mixing with your potable house water. You should also get approval from local utilities before digging to ensure that you don't cut into buried lines.

loss rate to compute the most effective watering schedule for your lawn and gardens on any given day. This is a big improvement given that most homeowners neglect their systems and only adjust them a few times a year, if that. An ET controller can adjust its rate 365 days a year.

ET controllers have significant water-saving potential. Recent studies conducted by municipalities concerned with water conservation show irrigation water savings of up to 30 percent. In addition to saving water, ET controllers are better for your lawns and landscape. They deliver the right amount of water. This means healthier turf and plants, fewer diseases, and fewer weeds.

Types of ET Controllers

There are two types of automated ET controllers on the market today. One uses an on-site weather monitor combined with input about your yard, such as soil type, ground slope, sprinkler types, and plant varieties. The other type of ET controller receives data from weather stations across North America. It uses this information, combined with input about the site, to determine ET rates. The Toro Company's Intelli-Sense controller, for example, utilizes satellite-relayed weather info about your locale and downloads it to the controller via a daily wireless page.

ET controllers cost more than those that rely primarily on rain sensors and homeowners—between $300 and $500. For homeowners on a budget, there are nonautomatic ET controllers that can improve a system's efficiency. They require more operator interaction but can also dramatically improve efficiencies. Toro's ECXTRA sprinkler timers, for example, include software (called The Toro Scheduling Advisor) that posts reminders on your computer about when to make adjustments to your watering program. On-screen questionnaires make it easy to update your site conditions. Based on your ZIP code, it calculates your home's longitude, latitude, and altitude and estimates ET rates.

Improved Sprinklers

Manufacturers have also tweaked the other end of home irrigation systems. Sprinkler heads have become easier to adjust and a lot more versatile. This

Ways to Reduce Watering

If you find your lawn dries out quickly and needs more frequent watering than other lawns in your neighborhood, here is a list of reminders to help you minimize waterings.

Keep your grass relatively tall. The plants will then help reduce evaporation by shading the soil. When possible, choose native grasses or those well adapted to your locale; they will need less watering. Bluegrass, for example, is a guzzler; Buffalograss is not. See Chapter 5 for more on grass types.

Improve your soil. This can also help reduce your watering needs. Try top-dressing your soil with organic material. Then work it into the soil using a core cultivator. Organic material helps your soil hold water longer. In addition, aeration promotes deeper root growth. When combined with infrequent, deep waterings, the deeper roots will enable grass plants to take moisture from a greater soil depth.

Choose the right fertilizers. How you fertilize and treat for pests and weeds significantly impacts your lawn's water requirements. The best advice is to keep chemicals off your lawn. Organic lawns require less watering than chemically treated lawns. You'll also save water if you do not overfertilize.

Use sharp mower blades. Cleanly cut lawns lose less moisture to evaporation. They look greener, too.

Follow nature's lead. When drought conditions persist, allow your lawn to temporarily brown-out or go dormant. This will not usually hurt a healthy lawn. There may be times during the year when it's just not worth trying to keep your lawn green.

Invest in timers. If you water your lawn manually, use a timer. With a timer, you can't forget to turn off the sprinkler. Caution: the ones that are programmable turn on rain or shine.

is good news for installers, whether they are contractors or do-it-yourselfers. No longer do you need to specify whether you want a quarter-arc, half-arc, or full-arc nozzle. You can make the adjustment on site. Newer sprinklers even allow you to change the angle of spray from low to high, or anywhere in between. This enables you to spray under and over ob-

Adjustable Sprinklers

THE ARC OF THIS ROTARY SPRINKLER HEAD CAN BE ADJUSTED BY THE HOMEOWNER WHEN THE NEED ARISES. TWIST THE COLLAR TO THE DESIRED SETTING.

SPRAY-TYPE HEADS CAN BE FINE-TUNED FOR ANY ANGLED PATTERN OF SPRAY. THE VERTICAL SPRAY ANGLES CAN ALSO BE ADJUSTED ON SOME MODELS.

ADJUSTING SPRAY PATTERNS AND ANGLE OF SPRAY IS DONE USING A SPECIAL TOOL SUPPLIED BY THE MANUFACTURER TO HELP AVOID TAMPERING.

stacles, such as low-hanging branches or fences. Once a system is installed, you will not need to make many spray head adjustments, but as plants grow, sprinkler head adjustability may again become a valuable feature.

For improved water conservation, matched precipitation nozzles are available from several manufacturers. These high-efficiency nozzles provide uniform coverage from sprinkler to sprinkler. Uneven coverage is a common cause of overwatering because sprinklers are commonly set for the head that is delivering the least amount of water.

One of the main causes of wasteful watering is a sprinkler that delivers inconsistent amounts of water. If one sprinkler in a zone delivers less than those around it, there will be a dry spot. The operator often compensates by running that zone for a longer period. In so doing, however, he will overwater elsewhere. New rotary sprinklers have precision-engineered nozzles that minimize brown spots and waste. Gear-driven, they deliver water slowly, so it has a chance to soak into the ground. They are also adjustable, so they can be custom fit to spraying arcs from 40 to 360 degrees. Interchangeable nozzles allow low-angle spray for avoiding obstacles.

Sensor Advances

Rain sensors have long been a recommended (and often mandated) accessory to lawn sprinkler systems. When it begins to rain, the sensor sends a signal to the controller to stop all watering. Some rain sensors are a bit smarter. They won't turn off until a significant amount of rain has fallen. With some of these, you can actually set the amount of rainfall needed to shut down the valves. The latest offerings include wireless rain sensors that reduce labor. Some wireless units are trickle charged with a photovoltaic solar cell. Others run on 9-volt batteries.

Manufacturers have recently added other types of sensors to their lines. Wind sensors signal the controller to cease watering when wind speeds reach levels that would cause unacceptable water loss. Similarly, freeze sensors cause systems to stop operating when air temperatures get close to freezing. Weather monitors, such as those used with ET controllers, can combine all of these functions.

HIGHER POP-UPS

Taller spray heads are now available, too. These 4-, 6-, and even 12-inch pop-up units do a better job of watering in high grass and ground-cover situations. Agronomists recommend higher lawn heights to improve a lawn's health, conserve water, and reduce the need for fertilizer, herbicides, and pesticides.

Hiring a Lawn Irrigation Contractor

The general advice for hiring construction contractors applies to hiring lawn-irrigation contractors as well. You should solicit bids from several, ask for references (and call them), ask to see insurance, and be sure you're comparing apples to apples when making your decision. You should also hire someone with experience—it's very easy to put in a system that will be plagued with problems and not so easy to fix once everything is buried.

There are a few other things to keep in mind. If you have done your research and are convinced you want to use a particular manufacturer's equipment, you may have a difficult time finding a willing installer. Most irrigation contractors choose one brand and then stick to it. They know how to make it work and don't have to stock spare parts for repairs from lots of different manufacturers. Most manufacturers' Web sites have links that will help match you with a contractor that uses their components.

Many residential irrigation contractors are experienced enough to size up your yard and design a system in their heads. Nevertheless, insist on a plan from each contractor bidding for your job. You may have to pay for it, but it will help avoid disputes and confusion later.

Finally, ask your contractor what he charges for maintenance and repair. Many homeowners have the installer start up their systems in the spring and shut them down in the fall. Some request additional visits for reprogramming and for repair. It's a good idea to know what these costs will be beforehand.

Irrigation Alternatives

With some municipalities restricting the use of water due to scarcity, it's no wonder that some homeowners are seeking other ways to keep some green in their lives.

Xeriscaping. One approach is xeriscaping—planting low-water-use grasses and plants—and taking measures to conserve water. In a water-rich state, such as Connecticut, that might mean opting for a perennial rye or zoysia for the lawn and drought-resistant garden plants such as Black-Eyed Susan. Grouping plants according to need is another good strategy. In drier states, such as Arizona or Colorado, it may mean building berms to channel runoff to garden beds, planting drought-tolerant ornamental grasses, and reducing lawn sizes and replacing them with gravel or bark mulches.

Micro Irrigation. Another approach that irrigation system manufacturers are beginning to promote more heavily is drip or "micro" irrigation. These systems are more efficient in their use of water because they deliver water directly to the plant roots slowly, so very little is wasted on weeds, runoff, and evaporation. Delivery is via a network of plastic tubes. Drip irrigation systems are used primarily for plantings, such as shrubs and trees. Some, however, may be used for lawn irrigation. A network of drip lines are buried about 4 inches below grade. They can be controlled with automatic valves and controllers, similar to those used for aboveground systems.

Drip irrigation is often used to irrigate individual plants, planters, and garden beds, above. Subsurface systems for irrigating lawns are also available.

Repairs and Improvements

At this point, your lawn complements the design of your house and looks dense and deep green—just the way you've always wanted it. Problem is, life is full of unexpected surprises. There are often bumps in the road. If that "bump" is a stump, you'll need to remove it. Or perhaps you created the problem by applying a bit too much fertilizer or parking the car on the grass. Maybe your lawn is getting too little sun (or too much sun) for the type of grass that was planted, or too many visits from a certain odorous nocturnal mammal in search of food. Whatever the case may be, your lawn is vulnerable and bound to need repairs and improvements from time to time. This chapter fills you in on the lawn-related damage you may encounter on occasion and provides you with quick, easy ways to fix it.

THIN TREE CANOPIES TO ALLOW ENOUGH SUN FOR GRASS TO GROW SUCCESSFULLY.

Clean Up Fertilizer Spills

If you spill too much fertilizer on an area of your lawn, rake it or, better yet, vacuum it using a shop vacuum, and water the affected area heavily. Unfortunately there isn't much you can do for a lawn already burned by mistakenly applying too much fertilizer except to water, wait, and overseed in the upcoming planting season. To be safe, take a soil sample of the browned area, and compare it with soil taken from a healthy area. If tests indicate the salts are still too high, consider postponing replanting. Or remove the sod and a couple inches of soil; add new soil; and patch as described below.

Patch Bare Spots

Patching bare spots is best done in the fall in the North, when weed competition is less intense, and so roots of reseeded areas have time to develop before summer. Begin by removing the existing damaged sod (extending several inches into

Patching a Bare Spot

1 BARE SPOTS CAN OCCUR FOR MANY REASONS, INCLUDING PETS AND LEAVING SOMETHING ON THE LAWN FOR SEVERAL DAYS.

2 TO REPAIR A SPOT WHERE THE GRASS HAS DIED, LOOSEN THE SOIL TO A DEPTH OF **6** TO **8** IN.

3 LEVEL THE SOIL USING A GARDEN RAKE, AND REMOVE ALL DEBRIS.

4 EVENLY SPREAD A MIXTURE OF FERTILIZER, SEED, AND SOIL OVER THE AFFECTED AREAS.

5 TO FIRM THE RESEEDED AREA, TAMP IT WITH A GARDEN RAKE. FOR LARGER AREAS, ROLL IT WITH A ROLLER THAT IS ONE-THIRD FULL.

the surrounding healthy area) and loosening the soil to a depth of 6 to 8 inches using a garden fork. Add a small amount of compost to the soil; level using an iron rake; and then reseed. It will help to lightly rake the seed into the soil and cover with a light (50 to 60 percent) layer of shredded straw mulch. Unlike hay sold for livestock, shredded straw does not have weed seeds in it, so the resulting grass patch will contain only what was in the seed mix. Patching mixes, consisting of seed, fertilizer, and mulch, are available at most garden centers and are convenient for patching small areas. For larger patches, lay on strips of sod and trim the edges to fit the bare area. Sod is also preferable to seed when patching in the spring and summer because weeds would overrun seedlings, and new roots don't have time to develop before the summer heat. You may also patch with plugs. Plant them in holes about 6 inches apart. Use a sod-plugging tool, an auger inserted into a cordless drill for planting bulbs, a trowel, or small spade to dig the holes. If you are handy you could make a template using the proper size dowel for your plug—mount these on a piece of plywood with screws, and press into the area needing to be patched. This will save you loads of time! Another nice thing about this template is that it can be used over and over again to create the correct spacing and exact size holes quickly. You can use the template to plant other things as well—not just plugs of grass! Dampen the plugs and soil before planting. In the South, repair dead lawn areas in the spring because warm-weather grasses need warm weather to grow well. Daily watering is critical for all newly patched areas.

• •

Did You Know? *According to the Environmental Protection Agency, more fuel is spilled each year filling up garden equipment than was lost in the entire Exxon Valdez oil spill in Alaska in 1989. Add gas or oil to your lawn mower on a flat, dry surface (a driveway or sidewalk, for example)—NOT when it's on the lawn.*

Repair Damage from Pets

Most lawn burn, caused by high levels of nitrogen in a dog's urine and feces, will repair itself over time, especially if a lawn is healthy and neither over- nor under-fertilized. To speed the healing process, flood the area with water or apply a product designed to neutralize the nitrogen, such as Dogonit. In some cases you must patch the damaged area by removing the damaged turf and preparing a seed bed by loosening the soil; then re-seed, sod, or with certain grasses, especially in the South, plant sprigs or plugs. You can also use special patching formulas that contain a mix of seed and mulch. Preventive steps include changing your pet's diet (if your dog is the cause) and replanting with more urine-resistant grasses, such as perennial rye-grasses and fescues.

Fix Damage from Skunks

If your lawn has spots where the sod is rolled back or spots where numerous 1-inch-diameter holes appear overnight, skunks may be the culprits. This usually happens in the fall, when the skunks search for grubs as they try to fatten up for the winter. It's usually too late at this point to get rid of the grubs, but take steps the following spring to get rid of the skunk if he has taken up residence under a deck, shed, or other structure. You can treat your lawn to prevent insects. There are a variety of natural grub killers. Use nematodes, milky spore disease, and others before treating with pesticides, which may be harmful to honeybees, humans, and pets. (See "Natural Controls," pages 160.) You should also keep garbage cans tightly lidded. If skunks persist, use motion-activated lights or sprinklers to discourage them from frequenting your yard.

Remove Unsightly, Weedy Edges

Ragged, poorly maintained borders between lawns and planting beds are breeding grounds for weeds. In addition to making a simple edge cut using a manual or power edger, there are metal and plastic edging products that are easy to install. Aluminum edging won't rust, and it bends easily to follow curves. It outlasts plastic and results in a cleaner-looking edge. To install: cut a vertical edge using a

Installing Edging

MASONRY EDGING HELPS KEEP THE LAWN OUT OF GARDEN BEDS, BUT IT DOESN'T ALLOW CLOSE MOWING.

PLASTIC EDGING IS EASY TO INSTALL BUT, DEPENDING ON HEIGHT, MAY REQUIRE THE USE OF A TRIMMER.

FLUSH, FLAT-SURFACE EDGING OF BRICK, LEFT, CONCRETE, OR WOOD TIMBERS WILL ALLOW YOU TO RUN MOWER WHEELS RIGHT OVER IT.

ALUMINUM EDGING IS A BIT MORE DIFFICULT TO INSTALL THAN PLASTIC EDGING, BUT IT IS ALSO LESS LIKELY TO PUSH UP OUT OF THE GROUND.

flat spade or a hand or power edger; position the edging so the top is about ½ inch above the soil. Position the edging's stake slots (if any) to the inside. Drive stakes, spaced as directed by the maker.

Flat-surface edging made of severe-weather brick creates a low-maintenance edge that mower wheels can ride on. (No string trimming required!) Dig a 1-foot-wide x 9-inch-deep trench. Shovel in 4 inches of well-tamped crushed stone for drainage. Top that with about 2 inches of tamped sand, and lay bricks so that the brick is about ½ inch above grade.

Let in the Sun

You should prune and thin trees and shrubs that affect the amount of sun your lawn gets. If your grass isn't getting enough sun, it won't look good even if the soil is in great condition and the lawn is well watered and fertilized. While some homeowners are equipped to handle tree-climbing tasks, most are not and should seek a qualified professional landscape contractor or professional arborist. Still, light pruning is well within the skill level of most homeowners.

Improper pruning can damage trees and shrubs, so review the guidelines shown here before you begin. When pruning deciduous tree branches larger than 1 inch in diameter, make cuts just above the branch bark ridge area, that looks like a "collar" where the branch meets the limb—this is the raised ridge of bark where the branch joins the trunk. This helps the tree to seal its own wound. Use the three-cut technique on heavy branches to prevent stripping bark from the trunk as the branch falls—and don't apply paint or other forms of dressing to the wound. Recent research has shown that applying a dressing may actually promote tree decay by sealing in harmful

HANDLING CONTOURS

To accommodate grade changes when installing aluminum or plastic edging, cut upside-down V-shaped notches into the edging's bottom edge, making it easier to bend the edging. Build up soil to the same height on the bed side as you go, and tamp it well.

Make Way for Sunshine

USE A TELESCOPING PRUNING SAW TO THIN UPPER TREE BRANCHES. USE THE BUILT-IN LOPPING SHEARS FOR SMALL BRANCHES.

WHEN PRUNING BACK SHRUBS AND TREES, CUT CLOSE TO AND AT THE ANGLE OF A BUD TO PREVENT DAMAGE TO THE BRANCH.

Good! Cut saves branch collar.

Bad! Cut too close to trunk.

WHEN PRUNING LARGE TREE BRANCHES AT THE TRUNK, CUT TO THE OUTER EDGE OF THE BRANCH COLLAR, ABOVE LEFT, TO PROMOTE HEALING.

TO AVOID STRIPPING BARK FROM A TREE WHEN THE CUT LIMB FALLS, UNDERCUT THE LIMB AT CUT 1, A FOOT AWAY FROM THE FINAL CUT. MAKE A TOP CUT A LITTLE FARTHER OUT AT CUT 2. MAKE THE FINAL CUT AFTER MOST OF THE BRANCH HAS FALLEN AWAY.

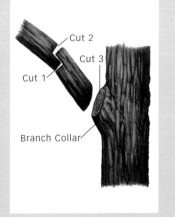

Cut 2

Cut 3

Cut 1

Branch Collar

Improve Grading

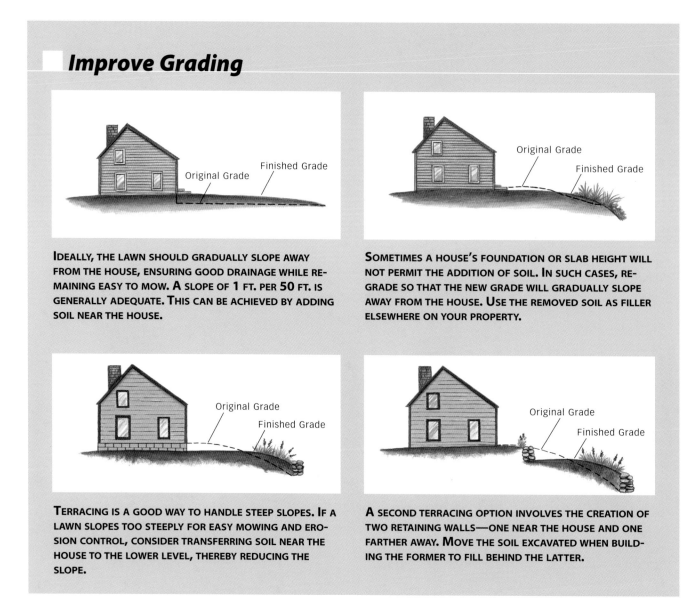

IDEALLY, THE LAWN SHOULD GRADUALLY SLOPE AWAY FROM THE HOUSE, ENSURING GOOD DRAINAGE WHILE REMAINING EASY TO MOW. A SLOPE OF 1 FT. PER 50 FT. IS GENERALLY ADEQUATE. THIS CAN BE ACHIEVED BY ADDING SOIL NEAR THE HOUSE.

SOMETIMES A HOUSE'S FOUNDATION OR SLAB HEIGHT WILL NOT PERMIT THE ADDITION OF SOIL. IN SUCH CASES, REGRADE SO THAT THE NEW GRADE WILL GRADUALLY SLOPE AWAY FROM THE HOUSE. USE THE REMOVED SOIL AS FILLER ELSEWHERE ON YOUR PROPERTY.

TERRACING IS A GOOD WAY TO HANDLE STEEP SLOPES. IF A LAWN SLOPES TOO STEEPLY FOR EASY MOWING AND EROSION CONTROL, CONSIDER TRANSFERRING SOIL NEAR THE HOUSE TO THE LOWER LEVEL, THEREBY REDUCING THE SLOPE.

A SECOND TERRACING OPTION INVOLVES THE CREATION OF TWO RETAINING WALLS—ONE NEAR THE HOUSE AND ONE FARTHER AWAY. MOVE THE SOIL EXCAVATED WHEN BUILDING THE FORMER TO FILL BEHIND THE LATTER.

microorganisms or other harmful pathogens. When pruning small branches, always prune back to a bud or to another branch. Always make the cut at the angle of the bud or remaining branch, taking care not to injure either one.

The best time to prune most live branches is in late winter or very early spring, when most trees and shrubs are dormant and before new growth starts. Pruning at this time promotes better healing and enables the plant to send out new growth the following spring. Avoid pruning trees producing high amounts of sap, such as maples and birches, after January. If necessary, trees can be pruned in summer or fall, but be sure to keep summer pruning moderate because that's when sap-producing trees and most plants are producing food. In general, avoid pruning in the spring. Dead wood can be removed at any time of the year, and the tree will usually benefit from it.

Remove Stumps

Removing small stumps (up to 10 inches in diameter) using a spade and ax is called grubbing. This requires strength and perseverance. First, dig a 1- to 2-foot-wide trench around the stump, 1 to 2 feet deep. As you encounter roots, expose and cut them, using a pruning saw, lopping shears, or ax. Continue to dig until you can insert a steel bar or shovel under the mass of roots. Pry on all sides, and continue to dig and cut newly exposed roots. On a tree with a significant taproot, you may need to dig deeper. Lean the root mass to one side, and cut the taproot as deep as possible. The stump will gradually break loose from the soil. For quick removal of larger stumps, rent a stump grinder or hire a tree-removal professional.

Repair Damage from Vehicles

Soil compaction caused by parked vehicles limits the amount of oxygen and water that gets to the lawn's roots, reducing its rooting depth and generally slowing growth. Aeration is the answer. Aerators remove cores of soil and deposit them on the surface. Foot aerators would only be effective on small areas, but for large areas, use an aerating machine (also called a core cultivator) that is driven, pushed, or towed across the lawn using a lawn tractor. Explore options at a tool-rental center. For best results, aerate large areas in the late summer or early fall, when grass enters a period of vigorous growth and there is less weed competition, and always water well the day before. Break up cores with the back of a rake, or remove and add to the compost pile.

Solve Poor Drainage

Solving minor drainage problems is something most homeowners can do. The most common drainage problem is water that runs off steep slopes, roofs, and driveways. Water that runs across the surface of your lawn can erode soil and wash away any grass that's trying to establish itself.

Redirect roof water. Roof water is commonly directed away from the house and basement by a system of fascia gutters and downspouts called leaders. If your lawn shows signs of erosion at the leaders, dig a trench about 2 feet deep x 3 feet wide x 6 feet long from the leader out into the lawn. Save any reusable sod. Then fill the trench with $1/4$-inch gravel to a depth of $1\frac{1}{2}$ feet, and cover with water-permeable landscape fabric and topsoil. The landscape fabric will keep the gravel bed from getting plugged with topsoil. Replant the affected area with sod or reseed it. Put a splash block, available at home centers, directly under the leader, or install a dry well under the leaders—a better alternative if you are dealing with a large volume of water.

Add a rain garden. A low-impact and environmentally sound solution would be to build a bio-retention area or rain garden to use the water. It would include plants that can sit in water for several hours while the area drains. This type of garden reduces the amount of runoff in storm water drains and is healthier for an area around a wetland.

Create a drip zone. For houses without gutters, experts recommend constructing a drip zone that begins under the roof eaves and extends several feet from the house. This zone is constructed similarly to the trench for a downspout described, except that this zone is usually filled with stones or gravel and covered with mulch.

Regrade. If the grade or slope of your land causes rainfall to flow toward your house or to low-lying areas where you are trying to grow grass or establish a garden, consult a landscape architect; solving drainage problems can be tricky. A professional will begin with percolation tests, which show areas that may need a subsurface drainage system. Lawns with steep slopes to the road (a drop greater than 1 foot over 50 feet) may be subject to bare spots resulting from erosion. They also waste rainwater by directing it to storm sewers before it can be absorbed by the soil. One solution is to use an oblong planting bed as a water trap. Placed at the foot of the slope, the bed will catch the runoff and, if well mulched, will rarely need watering.

CREATE A DRY WELL TO COLLECT RUNOFF FROM ROOF DOWNSPOUTS, HILLSIDES, OR PAVED AREAS. (THE PERFORATED BARREL'S SIDES ARE SHOWN CUT AWAY TO REVEAL ROCKS INSIDE.)

PART 3

SOLVING LAWN PROBLEMS

Controlling Weeds

Because weeds are survivors, designed to make a go of conditions that don't favor most other plants, they will always be with us, looking for a chance to establish themselves. Rather than cast a disparaging eye on anything growing in the lawn other than your chosen lawn grass, you are better off accepting that diversity is a fact of nature. Your task is to decide which weeds you can tolerate and which must go—whether because they are too noticeable, overly aggressive, or a health hazard. White clover, for example, was once considered a fashionable lawn plant. Pleasant to look at, it increased the nitrogen content of soils and helped to break up compaction. In more recent decades, it was classified as a weed because it doesn't look like grass. Today, as homeowners reconsider their definition of lawn weeds, clover is slowly regaining its status as a desirable lawn plant. Perhaps the best definition of weeds is simply a plant that's out of place. If you like the look of clover, then go for it!

SOME HOMEOWNERS CAN LIVE WITH CRABGRASS. OTHERS CAN'T. FORTUNATELY, THERE ARE NATURAL WAYS TO CONTROL IT .

Identifying Weed Species

To control weeds, you will first need to identify the various types growing in your turf. Weeds are either narrow-leaved and grass-like, or broad-leaved. You'll also need to know their life cycles so that you can effectively time your control measures.

Annual weeds are the most common, living for one growing season and reproducing only from seed. Cool-season annual weeds germinate in late fall or winter. They then flower, produce seeds, and die in the spring. They can be especially troublesome in dormant southern lawns, and that is why some people overseed with cool-season grass for the winter. Warm-season annuals go through their complete life cycle from the spring to the fall of the same year. These weeds are most problematic in northern grasses that go dormant in the summer heat.

Weed Invasions

SOME WEEDS LOOK MORE OUT OF PLACE THAN OTHERS, INCLUDING THIS PATCH OF DOLLAR WEED.

DETER ANNUAL CHICKWEED BY RAKING TO BRING UPRIGHT AND MOWING BEFORE THE PLANTS CAN SET SEED.

GROUND IVY, AN AGGRESSIVE WEED, SPREADS BY ABOVE-GROUND STOLONS AND BY UNDERGROUND RHIZOMES.

POORLY MAINTAINED BORDERS ARE BREEDING GROUNDS FOR WEEDS THAT EVENTUALLY INVADE YOUR LAWN.

The point to remember about annuals is that they reproduce only by seed, so they can be controlled by disrupting their growth any time before they set seed.

Perennial weeds are the long-lived ones. They don't die after flowering, and many reproduce both by seed and by vegetative means. Some perennial weeds, such as dandelions, have fleshy taproots that can produce a new plant from just a piece of root left in the ground. Creeping kinds, such as ground ivy, spread from underground rhizomes and above-ground stolons. Perennials are more difficult to eradicate, but they are as vulnerable during their seedling stage as the annuals.

Did You Know? *According to the Gardening Trends Research Report (April 2007), weed and insect control are the top two activities Americans planned for their lawns in 2007.*

Weeding Methods

SHALLOW-ROOTED WEEDS CAN BE LOOSENED USING A WEEDING TOOL AND THEN PULLED OUT.

YOU CAN ALSO SPOT-KILL SHALLOW-ROOTED WEEDS WITH BOILING WATER. WEAR HEAVY GLOVES TO PREVENT GETTING SCALDED.

PRY SLIGHTLY USING A SPADE TO LOOSEN THE SOIL AROUND A DEEP-ROOTED WEED, AND GRASP AT THE BASE.

PULL SLOWLY. IT IS IMPORTANT TO PULL OUT THE ENTIRE ROOT. MOISTENED SOIL WILL EASE THE CHORE.

FIGHTING WITH FIRE

Smart TIP

Organic farmers have successfully used fire to kill weeds. "Flaming" is done with a gas torch that emits a narrow flame. The object is to heat the plant's sap until its cell walls burst. Just the clear cone of gas surrounding the flame is actually passed across the foliage until it starts to soften and wilt. Because the roots aren't injured, you will need to repeat this treatment on perennials when the foliage regrows. Eventually the weed will use up its carbohydrate stores and be unable to reproduce or put out new growth. Use extra care when fighting with fire; be sure that no dry leaves, pine needles, or other dry plant material is near you at the time you are using the torch. Keep a hose or bucket of water nearby, just in case.

Cultural Measures Count

Mowing to the right height, as discussed in Chapter 7, is one key to preventing weeds. In addition to promoting healthier grass, keeping your turf on the long side helps block sunlight from weed seeds just waiting to germinate. When weed seeds are evident, catch your grass clippings and dispose of them, rather than redistributing them on the lawn. Maintaining optimal fertility is also paramount, as a dense lawn makes it difficult for weeds to compete. Critical, too, is the timing of fertilizer applications. Applying fertilizer in the summer to dormant northern grasses is a sure-fire way to energize any weeds present. On southern lawns, applying fertilizer in the fall encourages cool-season weed growth. Fertilize northern lawns in the fall and southern lawns in mid-spring to ensure strong growth as the grasses enter their main growing seasons. Another way to make life inhospitable for certain weeds is to rectify compaction and poor drainage. Lastly, thwart the growth of shallow-rooted weeds by watering deeply but infrequently, and allow the top ½ inch of soil to dry out between irrigations.

Weeds are opportunistic plants, and sometimes ridding your lawn of them entails changing those conditions conducive to their growth. Areas compacted from frequent foot traffic, and therefore prone to growing plantain and crabgrass, might be better served by the installation of a walkway or stepping-stones. If weeds congregate in hard-to-mow areas under or adjacent to fences and walls, consider eliminating them by using edging and mulches. If a bare area should develop, don't leave it open to weed invasion; reseed as soon as possible.

The Nitty-Gritty of Weed Removal

Although prevention through appropriate cultural methods is your first line of defense against weeds, there comes a time when you need to roll up your sleeves and get after them. On small areas, the old-fashioned approach is still the best—pull them out by hand. Make weeding a regular part of your maintenance routine, completed in the cool of the day when the soil is damp. Hand weeding may take a bit longer than using selective herbicides, but it's a

Smart TIP

CONTROL WEEDS

Scientists are researching improved ways to control weeds. One method involves using fungi to attack targeted plants. Called mycoherbicides, these fungi and other naturally occurring compounds show promise for inhibiting weeds. Research is also focused on allelopathic grasses, such as perennial ryegrasses and tall fescues, which have properties that cause them to make soils inhospitable to certain weeds. As new cultivars come out, look for those that can be overseeded into your lawn to offer a measure of protection against certain weeds.

lot better than worrying about the kids and pets getting into the toxic compounds that you must otherwise use and then safely store. Besides, if you add up the time it takes to drive to the nursery to buy the herbicides, to wash down the applicator, to study the directions and mix the proper solution, to apply the proper solution, and, as often as not, to bring expired herbicides to facilities for proper disposal, you will find that the no-herbicide approach doesn't take much more time, if any. If it has been excessively dry, you might want to water first to make it easier to pull the weeds.

Weeds with shallow, fibrous roots, such as chickweed, yield well to pulling. Grip them as close to the soil as possible, and then rock them back and forth to loosen them before giving a yank. Success in digging out weeds with taproots depends on getting the entire root. Ideally, these perennials should be removed as seedlings, when they are less firmly rooted. But in reality, we frequently don't notice them until the lawn turns yellow with blossoms.

For larger, established plants, using a spade works well, but smaller plants can easily be taken care of with a long-handled prong-type weeder. This tool, or a pointed trowel, is also quite useful when popping weeds that have a rosette of leaves right at ground level, such as plantains and other compact weeds.

Herbicides

When looking at large areas of lawn contaminated by weeds, most people consider resorting to herbicides. In fact, it is difficult to go to a local garden supply store without seeing shelves of products all promising to quickly rid your lawn of weed problems. Unfortunately, herbicides toxic to your weeds are often hazardous to your health, and to the health of other living things that come into contact with them. Certain components of herbicides, such as the chemicals 2,4-D and arsenic, may pose serious health hazards and are under scrutiny. Many herbicides do not break down quickly but remain active in the soil, increasing both health and contamination risks.

What is a beleaguered homeowner to do? If you cannot avoid using herbicides, look for the least toxic products and spot-treat affected areas only. Avoid products containing controversial chemicals, such as 2,4-D. Look also for formulations that break down rapidly in sunlight and by microbial action; such products do not leave chemical residues that can be tracked into the house. Unfortunately, many of the rapidly biodegradable solutions now available are nonselective. This means that any foliage that comes in contact with them, including your turf-grasses, will be injured or killed off. These products are appropriate only for spot-treating weeds in the lawn or for use along fence lines, walls, and other structures.

The Environmental Protection Agency (EPA) tests and rates the toxicity of all herbicides, requiring that one of four "signal" words be used as warnings on labels. They are, from most to least toxic: I. DANGER; II. WARNING; III. CAUTION; IV. CAUTION. Signal words for the same formulation may vary with the degree of concentration. Use any herbicide, no matter how mild, with great care and never

THE USE OF AN HERBICIDE TO SPOT-TREAT HARD-TO-WEED AREAS IS SOMETIMES NECESSARY.

when it's windy; always follow label directions strictly. Look for herbicides made of naturally occurring products, such as fatty acids, that are quickly decomposed by soil microorganisms. Do not, under any circumstances, increase the amount of herbicide used to kill an area quicker; this is irresponsible behavior and could result in a large fine from the Department of Environmental Protection.

Common Lawn Weeds

Here are the most common weeds and recommended means of dealing with them.

Annual bluegrass (Poa annua)

Frequently found in compacted, infertile soils, this light green, low-growing grassy annual prefers cool-season growth but can be found all year. Sudden lawn brown-out with the heat of summer or prolific seed production in spring signals its presence. When seed appears, rake the grass upright, and then mow and bag clippings.

Crabgrass (Digitaria species)

Few summer lawns are without this warm-season annual that branches out its low-growing, wide leaves. There are two varieties: the more upright is called large, or hairy, crabgrass; the more prostrate type is called smooth, or small, crabgrass. The latter

Some Least-Toxic Herbicides

Herbicidal Soap (by Safer: saferbrand.com) is made from potassium salts of fatty acids derived from naturally occurring plant oils and animal fats. Contact with herbicidal soap damages plant cell walls, causing dehydration and tissue death. Soaps are broad-spectrum, nonselective, and work best on seedlings. Deep-rooted weeds and perennials will require repeat applications. Soaps break down completely within 48 hours and carry an EPA rating of IV. CAUTION. There is also an herbicidal soap for use specifically on lawn moss.

Glyphosate (Roundup: roundup.com; KleenUp by Bonide Products, Inc.: bonideproducts.com) is a water-soluble salt that inhibits a plant's ability to produce certain essential amino acids, thus hindering new growth. This is a nonselective, broad-spectrum herbicide with an EPA rating of IV. CAUTION. Glyphosate is biodegradable and not harmful to life in the soil, where it has an average half-life of less than 45 days. Effects may not be seen for 7 to 10 days.

Glufosinate-Ammonium (Finale by Bayer Crop-Science: bayercropscience.com), a metabolic compound originally derived from a soil bacterium, interferes with photosynthesis, killing annual weeds and even many perennial weeds in one to four days. While nonselective and broad-spectrum, it affects only those plants that have been treated. It is biodegradable with an average half-life in soil of 7 to 20 days. It carries an EPA rating of III. CAUTION.

Weed-A-Way (by Safer) is an example of a selective, broad-leaved weed herbicide that does not contain 2,4-D. Broadleaf weeds will begin to curl in three or four days. It includes a colorant that allows you to see where you've sprayed to help prevent overapplication. It carries an EPA rating of IV. CAUTION.

---

has purplish stems. Both types produce prolific seed heads that stand out like long fingers. Mowing high, removing seed heads, and maintaining dense turf are essential to its control.

Purslane (Portulaca oleracea)

Forming reddish mats of succulent oblong leaves and stems, this warm-season annual likes hot, dry weather. Its fibrous root system allows for fairly easy pulling, but don't leave any stem fragments behind because they are capable of developing new roots. The plant bears small yellow flowers followed by urn-shaped capsules that release tiny black seeds.

Prostrate spurge (Euphorbia prostrata)

Prominent in summer, this warm-season annual grows in rosettes of green, hairy-leaved stems. A related variety, spotted spurge (*E. maculata*), is similar but has a purple leaf spot. Generally low-growing with a taproot, prostrate spurge exudes a milky sap from broken stems.

Annual chickweed (Stellaria species)

Delicate in appearance, this low-growing annual may remain green all year in mild climates.

Corn gluten meal, SOLD UNDER VARIOUS BRAND NAMES, IS AN EFFECTIVE WAY TO CONTROL CRABGRASS, DANDELION, PURSLANE, BLACK NIGHTSHADE, COMMON LAMBQUARTERS, CREEPING BENTGRASS, CURLY CLOCK, REDROOT PIGWEED, AND OTHER TYPES OF WEEDS. IT IS A PREEMERGENT HERBICIDE THAT WORKS BY INHIBITING ROOT FORMATION. THE TIMING OF APPLICATION IS CRITICAL. IDEALLY, IT SHOULD BE APPLIED THREE TO FIVE WEEKS BEFORE THE TARGET WEEDS GERMINATE, TYPICALLY IN MID-TO-LATE SPRING. CORN GLUTEN MEAL, WHICH IS **10** PERCENT NITROGEN, ALSO SERVES AS A SLOW-RELEASE FERTILIZER.

Preferring shade and areas of thin grass, it can be distinguished from its perennial cousin by its small, heart-shaped, bright-green leaves and petite white flowers that resemble stars. Pulling, raking to bring it upright, and mowing all help to deter it.

Perennial chickweed (Cerastium vulgatum)
Also called mouse ear for the shape of its hairy, dark green leaves, this perennial forms dense mats of low growth. It spreads by seeds and creeping rootstocks, and prefers infertile soil. Digging up, raking upright, and mowing help keep this perennial in check.

Ground ivy (Glechoma hederacea)
Because of its vigorous growth, this one-time ground cover is now considered a hard-to-control weed. A cool-season perennial, ground ivy has rounded leaves with scalloped edges growing along square stems. It thrives in moist shade but spreads readily in the sun as well. Harbingers of later seed, lavender to blue funnel-shaped flowers appear in early spring. At the first sign of growth, pull or hoe up plants. Rake upright in spring, and mow close.

Dandelion (Taraxacum officinale)
The bright yellow flowers of this cool-season perennial soon turn to delicate spheres of seeds. Dandelions bloom from spring to frost, with new seedlings appearing in the fall. It's best to dig out the fleshy taproot when the plant is in flower and consequently low on the carbohydrate reserves needed for regrowth. Weeding when the ground is moist will make your job easier.

Common plantain (Plantago major)
Rosettes of waxy green leaves appear, especially in dry, compacted lawns. This cool-season perennial spreads both by new shoots and seed formed on

Common Weeds

ANNUAL BLUEGRASS (*POA ANNUA*)

CRABGRASS (*DIGITARIA* SPECIES)

PURSLANE (*PORTULACA OLERACEA*)

PROSTRATE SPURGE (*EUPHORBIA PROSTRATE*)

SPOTTED SPURGE (*E. MACULATA*)

ANNUAL CHICKWEED (*STELLARIA* SPECIES)

seed heads resembling rat tails. Low mowing and poor fertility encourage growth.

Buckhorn plantain (Plantago lanceolata)

Also a cool-season perennial, this plantain has long, slender leaves with three to five prominent veins. Arising from a rosette of leaves with a taproot, the seed heads look like short cylinders atop long spikes. To discourage, alleviate compaction; improve fertility; and raise mowing height.

Nimbleweed (Muhlenbergia schreberi)

Showing up in late spring, this warm-season grassy perennial becomes obvious when it turns straw-colored in early fall. Its leaves branch off fine, wiry stems that contrast with surrounding grasses. Spread by stolons and a shallow, fibrous root system, it prefers hot, dry conditions and either forms circular patches or appears throughout a lawn.

Smart TIP

YOUR BEST DEFENSE

Some gardeners consider weed control a type of battle to be won. Another approach is to regard weeds as a warning that all is not well with your lawn and to take steps to improve conditions. Keeping your lawn growing vigorously by providing an optimal growing environment will help minimize weeds and prevent other problems. When weeds do creep in, you need to identify the conditions or practices encouraging their growth.

PERENNIAL CHICKWEED (*CERASTIUM VULGATUM*)

GROUND IVY (*GLECHOMA HEDERACEA*)

DANDELION SEED HEAD (*TARAXACUM OFFICINALE*)

COMMON PLANTAIN (*PLANTAGO MAJOR*)

BUCKHORN PLANTAIN (*PLANTAGO LANCEOLATA*)

NIMBLEWILL (*MUHLENBERGIA SCHREBERI*)

Fighting Lawn Diseases

Keeping your lawn healthy is a matter of sticking to basic management practices more so than looking to chemical solutions. The importance of paying attention to mowing height, aeration, drainage, irrigation, and fertilization really can't be stressed enough. Coupling these practices with the use of suitable grass cultivars and healthy soil will give your lawn an advantage over the harmful microorganisms normally found in most yards.

Fortunately, it takes more than the presence of pathogens (disease-causing microorganisms) to bring on infection in lawns. You also need a host—that is, a grass susceptible to a particular pathogen—and environmental conditions that foster disease. Conditions favoring pathogens vary but generally include warm weather and extended periods of moisture from rain, humidity, irrigation, or poor drainage. Other conditions, such as drought and high heat, encourage problems because they reduce the grass's ability to fight off infection. These three elements—pathogen, host, and environment—make up the "Plant Disease Triangle." Any one factor on its own cannot initiate disease. Problems begin when all three come together.

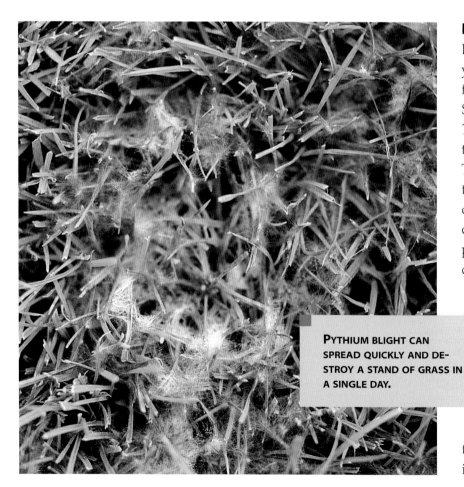

PYTHIUM BLIGHT CAN SPREAD QUICKLY AND DESTROY A STAND OF GRASS IN A SINGLE DAY.

Fungi: Friends and Foes

Dwelling in your soil and upon your lawn are myriad thread-like forms of plant life called fungi. Some of these fungi, such as *Trichoderma harzianum,* are important components of healthy soil. They may facilitate nutrient uptake by grasses and keep disease-causing fungi in check through competition for resources. The problems arise when the disease-causing group becomes dominant.

The initiators of most lawn diseases, these fungi are spread by wind, rain, grass clippings, and even your mower. They can overwinter and remain dormant in soil or thatch for long periods of time, awaiting just the right conditions before growing. Like a person, your lawn

Know What to Look For

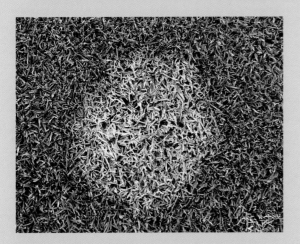

Pink snow mold's SCATTERED SPOTS CONTRAST CLEARLY WITH DORMANT TURF.

Fairy rings ARE RINGS OF DARK GREEN GRASS, OFTEN ACCOMPANIED BY A RING OF MUSHROOMS. GRASS IN THE CENTER OF THE RINGS OFTEN WITHERS.

Stripe smut RESULTS IN POOR GROWTH AND LONG, YELLOW-GREEN GRASS BLADE STREAKS THAT TURN BLACK.

becomes a target for infection if stressed. Although you cannot keep pathogens off your grass, you can sidestep disease by manipulating the other two factors: host and environment.

To keep your lawn from becoming a host, choose the right grass for a given location, and keep it healthy. Given the wide range of disease-resistant grasses available today, you have a good chance of avoiding certain diseases right from the start. (See Chapter 5 for more information on disease-resistant grasses.)

You might not be able to change the weather, but you can lessen its negative impact on your grass. Well-aerated lawns with good drainage and air circulation will experience fewer moisture problems. In areas prone to brown patch, some homeowners remove the morning dew (which contains nutrient sugars that contribute to brown patch formation) by lightly hosing down the lawn or pulling a hose across it. Good cultural practices do make a difference in the health of a lawn.

Ironically, often the very actions we take to improve our lawns aid in the establishment of diseases. For example, frequent light waterings encourage shallow root growth, making the grass vulnerable to drought stress. Watering late in the day leaves a wet grass canopy that is conducive to fungal growth. Also, excessive use of high-nitrogen fertilizer promotes unnecessarily lush top-growth that is more prone to disease. And using a dull mower blade shreds grass tips, providing a potential entry point for infection.

● ● ● ● ● ● ● ● ● ● ● ● ● ● ● ● ● ●

Did You Know?
The term "fairy ring," which dates back to 1599, comes from the folk belief that such rings were caused by fairies or pixies dancing in a circle, wearing out the grass.

THE GRASS IN THE "BULL'S-EYE," ABOVE, WAS KILLED BY REPEATED SPRAYS OF URINE FROM THE GUILTY PARTY, TOP. EXCESS NITROGEN FROM THE URINE FORCED THE SURROUNDING GRASS OUT OF DORMANCY IN EARLY SPRING, PRODUCING THE CIRCULAR TUFT OF LUSH, DEEP GREEN GRASS.

Is It Really Disease?

The best time to assess your turf's state of health is before mowing. While you are out picking up fallen twigs or removing other items from the lawn, stop to take a careful look at any areas that appear wilted or off-color or that otherwise stand out from their surroundings. If you do note changes, don't rush to blame them on disease; there are numerous other possibilities. For instance, a general browning-out of a cool-season grass during high summer is likely just summer dormancy, the grass's protective response to drought and heat. Dull, wilted, bluish-gray turf is the grass's signal that it needs water. General yellowing and stunted growth may be attributable to a lack of iron or nitrogen. Ragged leaf tips and a whitish cast usually indicate that your mower blades need sharpening.

Consider also the kinds of activities that have recently occurred in your yard. Perhaps the bright green rings surrounding dead grass are courtesy of the neighbor's dog, and the brown patches near the garage could be the result of a gasoline spill. While problems, these eyesores are limited in scope and can usually be rectified with fertilization, irrigation, or spot reseeding. If your turf's decline cannot be explained by such causes, look more closely.

Identifying Diseases

Many diseases will leave you with bleached-out dead turf. If you have reached this point, then you have not only lost the grass but also the opportunity to determine what caused the problem. Diseases are progressive in nature, especially during hot, humid weather. It's important to observe your lawn regularly if you want to spot disease symptoms that are apparent only early on. Look for spots or banding, color changes, or signs of decay on grass blades. When you examine affected turf, ask yourself some questions. What is its shape, size, and color? Does it feel slimy or dry? If there are patches, how are they distributed across the lawn? Give the grass a tug to check for rot. Lastly, venture out early in the morning while the lawn is damp with dew to look for signs of fungal mycelia. These fine, cobweb-like threads disappear with the day's heat and sun.

Identifying lawn diseases can be difficult. Damage

may not be apparent until turf is stressed by drought and heat. If your lawn's symptoms stump you, take a sample to a reputable nursery, a Cooperative Extension Service lab, or your state university plant-pathology department. Before taking samples, be sure to call and obtain specific sampling instructions.

When disease does get a foothold in your lawn, you need to take immediate steps to contain it. Start by bagging your lawn clippings and not adding them to your compost pile. Next, avoid walking through infected turf, especially when it's wet. Now is the time to review your management practices to determine why your grass became susceptible. Then decide which actions are needed to improve your lawn's growth environment and to alleviate the conditions that foster fungal growth. Keep in mind that as weather conditions change, they may no longer promote fungal growth, thereby allowing the problem to resolve itself naturally. But if disease symptoms continue, you may decide that you need to apply a fungicide. (See page 150.)

Grass cultivars named on the following pages are just a sampling of available grasses with resistance to various diseases.

Spring-Through-Fall Lawn Diseases

Fairy rings

Caused by more than 50 varieties of fungus, the rings vary in size and appearance but all form in soil that is high in woody, organic matter, usually from buried debris or tree stumps.

Look for: Rings of fast-growing, dark-green grass with centers of weeds, thin turf, or dead grass. Midsummer and fall rings are more apt to be composed of dead grass.

Management: The rings are difficult to remove unless completely dug out to a minimum depth of 1 foot. Aerating the ring area to improve water penetration and fertilizing to minimize color variation are helpful.

Stripe Smut

The disease causes yellowed, stunted growth in 6- to 12-inch patches.

Look for: Development of characteristic black stripes

Top-Dressing with Compost

Research has shown that microorganisms present in well-aged (at least one year old) organic compost can suppress turfgrass diseases. Scientists at Cornell University note that effective control of dollar spot, brown patch, and gray snow mold can be achieved with monthly applications of such "suppressive" compost. Additionally, regular top-dressing also lessens the severity of pythium blight and necrotic ring-spot infections.

Recommended suppressive top dressings include composted manures, pulverized tree bark, leaf compost, composted garden debris, sludge (such as Milorganite), and agricultural wastes. Top-dress with a ¼-inch layer of well-aged compost once in early spring and again in the fall. In addition to helping to fight disease, it may decrease your thatch layer and supply nutrients to your lawn. (See Chapter 2, pages 33 to 35, for more information about making and using compost.)

PATCHES OF PINK SNOW MOLD— CALLED FUSARIUM PATCH WHEN THE DISEASE STRIKES WITHOUT SNOW COVER— MAY START OFF ORANGE-BROWN AND TURN LIGHT GRAY BEFORE TURNING A SALMON COLOR.

Long-Term Practices That Help Prevent Disease

- *Choose recommended grass-seed mixtures. That way, if lawn disease does develop, not all grass types will be affected.*
- *Look for improved or disease-resistant cultivars when renovating or starting new lawns.*
- *Water your lawn early in the day, from sunrise until 11 a.m.*
- *Water only when needed, and then to a depth of 6 to 8 inches.*
- *Maintain adequate lawn aeration and drainage.*
- *Never cut off more than one-third of the grass length at one time.*
- *Keep mower blades sharp (below).*
- *Keep thatch to ½ inch in height.*
- *Apply appropriate fertilizer, and correct nutrient deficiencies, especially calcium.*
- *Prune and thin trees and tall shrubs to increase air circulation and sunlight exposure.*

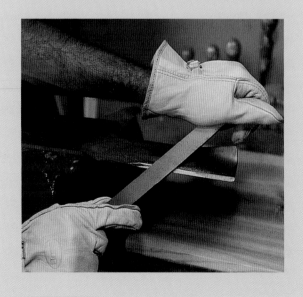

of erupted spores along grass blades that later become dry, shredded, and curled.

Management: Maintain adequate fertilization. Water well; mow frequently; and bag clippings. If the disease persists, stop wasting time and money on fungicides. Upgrade your lawn to a newer, disease-resistant cultivar instead. Consult your Cooperative Extension Service for the best cultivar for your locale.

Necrotic ring spot

Although the fungus is active during cool, moist periods, the damage frequently doesn't show until later, when turf is stressed.

Look for: Circular "frog-eye" patterns of 6 to 12 inches with matted, straw-colored grass surrounding a tuft of green grass. As infection advances, roots and crowns may turn brown to black. Thatch may decompose in affected areas, giving them a sunken, or "donut," appearance.

Management: Overseed with disease-resistant cultivars of tall fescue and perennial ryegrasses, or use bluegrasses. Water to lessen drought and heat stress. Avoid excessive fertilizer use. Remove excess thatch, and maintain adequate aeration and drainage.

Drechslera melting-out and leaf spot

Exhibiting two phases, the disease is especially destructive on overfertilized, lush bluegrasses. Cloudy, moist weather in the 70° to 85°F range brings on the telltale leaf-spot phase.

Look for: Distinctive dark purple spots that develop into buff-colored oval lesions with a dark brown or purple margin. Blades progress to yellow and then turn tan. During the melting-out phase, rot develops in roots and crowns.

Management: Avoid excessive nitrogen fertilizer; water infrequently but deeply; mow high; aerate; and remove excess thatch. If the disease persists, upgrade your lawn to a disease-resistant cultivar.

Summer Lawn Diseases

Brown patch

The disease is prevalent during moist, hot weather on overfertilized lawns.

Look for: Dark, water-soaked-looking grass turning to browned-out circular areas several inches to sev-

Damp-Condition Diseases

Fairy rings, CALLED DARK GRASS RINGS, MAY INCLUDE MUSHROOMS.

Stripe smut LEADS TO DRY, SHREDDED, CURLED GRASS BLADES.

Kentucky bluegrass IS PRONE TO NECROTIC RING SPOT.

Necrotic ring spot CAN BE CAUSED BY EXCESSIVE FERTILIZATION.

Dreschlera leaf spot IS FOSTERED BY EVENING WATERING.

A close-up look AT DRESCHLERA LEAF SPOT.

eral feet in diameter. Frequently some green leaves persist within the patch, and roots remain intact. Blades may have irregular ash gray lesions with a dark brown margin running along one side. On short turf, a 2-inch "smoke ring" of gray mycelium may encircle the patch in early morning.

Management: Water deeply but infrequently; mow high; remove excess thatch; and improve aeration and drainage.

Dollar spot

Affects low-nitrogen lawns, especially when stressed by drought and when heavy dews are prevalent.

Look for: Mottled, straw-colored 4- to 6-inch patches on lawns with taller grass. Grass blades have light tan bands with reddish brown margins spanning across them. Patches may merge to form large, irregular areas. Grayish white cobweb-like mycelium may be present in early morning.

Management: Maintain adequate nitrogen and potassium fertility; water deeply when necessary; and remove excess thatch. If your grass is prone to dollar spot, remove morning dew by dragging a hose across the lawn. Or overseed with a blend of improved cultivars.

Pythium blight

A serious, rapidly spreading disease involving the entire grass plant, pythium blight occurs on poorly drained soils that have a wet grass canopy. Look for it when nighttime temperatures plus relative humidity equals 150.

Look for: The sudden appearance of 1- to 6-inch reddish brown, wilted patches, which turn to streaks as they enlarge along drainage patterns. In early morning, the grass is slimy, dark, and matted. White

A Word About Fungicides

Fungicides have been the traditional means of treating lawn diseases. While fungicides do clear up certain problems, they unfortunately may make turf vulnerable to new ones. This happens primarily because fungicides kill off the beneficial, disease-suppressing microorganisms and fungi, as well as targeted organisms. If your disease symptoms continue unabated and you feel the need to use a fungicide, use it sparingly and follow the package directions. Of the mineral-based fungicides, elemental sulfur is considered the least toxic to humans and is available in a wide range of products.

Nonsulfuric, natural fungicides are also available. One is made with extract of neem oil. It controls rust and kills some insects. Another is 98 percent garlic juice! It's effective for controlling brown patch and dollar spot and is recommended for all types of grasses.

cottony mycelium may be present when grass is wet. As it dries, the grass turns light tan and shrivels.

Management: Improve drainage and air circulation; avoid overwatering; aerate; reduce excess thatch; and avoid nitrogen fertilizer during warm weather. Check calcium levels, and add lime if deficient. Observe closely for spread, and consult your Cooperative Extension Service if the disease progresses.

Rust

Appears on low-fertility, compacted, or shady lawns when growth slows during hot, dry weather.

Look for: Initial small yellow flecks that develop into pustules releasing yellow, orange, red, or dark brown spores. From a distance the turf appears orange or yellow, and colored spore residue rubs off if touched.

Management: Provide appropriate fertilization and irrigation; prune low-hanging tree branches to reduce shade; maintain aeration; and mow frequently, bagging clippings. Upgrade your lawn with a rust-resistant cultivar if the disease persists.

Fall-Through-Spring Lawn Diseases

Typhula blight (gray snow mold)

Strictly a cold-weather disease, typhula blight appears where snow cover has melted, especially in areas where snow has drifted or been piled.

Look for: Irregular 2- to 24-inch patches of bleached-out, matted turf covered with moldy, grayish white mycelium. Tiny black or orange-brown spherical sclerotia (hard fungus bodies) may be observed imbedded in the leaves and crowns of infected plants.

Management: Avoid heavy nitrogen fertilization in late fall to allow new growth time to harden off before winter. Keep thatch to a minimum and grass height lower as winter begins. Avoid piling snow onto your lawn, and prevent compaction on important turf areas by limiting activity on them when they're covered with snow. Rake in early spring to promote drying and reduce matting. Provide a light spring fertilization if damage is present.

Fusarium patch (pink snow mold)

This disease develops from late fall to early spring during cool, moist, cloudy weather, with or without snow cover.

Look for: Small, light tan to rusty brown circular patches that may grow to 2 feet and become ring-like as interior grass re-grows. When the grass is moist, salmon-colored mycelium is visible in sunlight. There are no sclerotia present.

Management: Fertilize in late fall, once grass growth ceases, with a slow-release nitrogen fertilizer. Mow the lawn; keep thatch low; and don't allow leaves or debris to remain on the lawn over winter. Rake the lawn well in early spring, and follow with a light fertilization if damage is present. As with any older, disease-prone lawn, consider upgrading to one of today's high-tech cultivars. You may be able to make a gradual transition by overseeding in successive years, or you may need to remove the existing turf for replanting.

Did You Know? *Fungi reproduce by microscopic particles called spores, which are spread by wind, water, people, animals, and tools such as lawn mowers and rakes.*

More Common Lawn Diseases

Brown patch, ALSO KNOWN AS RHIZOCTONIA BLIGHT, IS MOST ACTIVE WHEN GRASS REMAINS WET AND TEMPERATURES REACH **80** TO **90** DEG. F.

Dollar spot, NAMED AFTER THE SILVER-DOLLAR-SIZE SPOTS THAT FIRST APPEAR ON CLOSELY MOWED LAWNS, OFTEN SIGNALS A TURF THAT IS NUTRITIONALLY DEFICIENT.

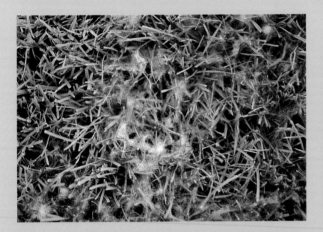

Pythium blight, ALSO KNOWN AS GREASE SPOT OR COTTONY BLIGHT, SPREADS RAPIDLY AND CAUSES DIE-OFF.

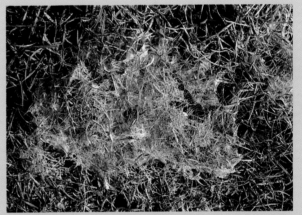

Gray snow molds ARE MORE APT TO DEVELOP WHEN EARLY, WET SNOW FALLS ON UNFROZEN GROUND.

Rust IS APTLY NAMED FOR THE COLOR YOUR GRASS TURNS WHEN THIS SELF-LIMITING DISEASE IS PRESENT.

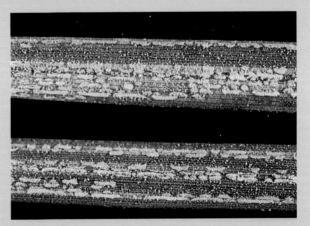

A closer look AT GRASS THAT HAS BEEN INFECTED WITH RUST SHOWS ORANGE, RED, BROWN, AND YELLOW SPORES THAT RUB OFF WHEN TOUCHED.

Managing Lawn Pests

Insect problems, like diseases, are apt to develop when conditions are favorable to them. As the weather warms up in spring, insect populations and activity increase. Your first and best line of defense against these pests is to provide optimal growing conditions for your lawn. The objective is to cultivate a thick, healthy turf that isn't overly attractive to pests as either habitat or food. Being more resilient, such lawns are also better able to survive the inevitable foraging of insects.

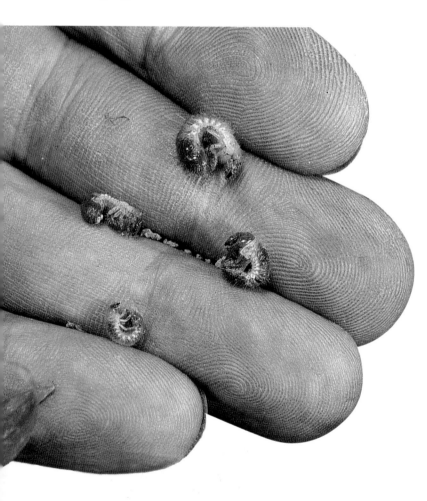

Japanese beetle larvae, OR GRUBS, ABOVE, ARE CONSIDERED THE SINGLE MOST DAMAGING LAWN PEST IN THE UNITED STATES. SHOWN AS AN ADULT, TOP.

Preventative Tactics

There was a time when lawn insects could count on finding a great meal just about anywhere they went. Today their pickings are far slimmer, thanks to new grass cultivars containing endophytic fungi that repel or kill insects attempting to eat them. Incorporating such grasses into existing lawns or planting new lawns with them will markedly cut down on problems resulting from ground-level pests.

Insects are also especially fond of the lush new growth typically found on highly fertilized lawns. Avoiding overfertilization and applying fertilizers at the right time will supply the necessary nutrients to your grass without fostering the fast, weak growth that is so attractive to pests. If and when the bugs do arrive, you can further thwart them by encouraging beneficial insect predators into your yard.

IPM, an Eco-Friendly Approach

For many years, insects in general have been viewed as invaders that should be attacked with various toxic chemicals. While such actions may take care of the immediate problem, they usually create a host of others. Today, an ecologically sound concept called Integrated Pest Management, or IPM, is receiving serious recognition

A LAWN ATTACKED BY GRUBS WILL HAVE PATCHES OF DEAD, DYING, OR WILTED GRASS. BUT IF INJURY IS MODERATE, THE LAWN MAY RECOVER.

and support among home gardeners, professional landscapers, and scientists. With IPM, the yard is viewed as an ecosystem with components that are interdependent and where every action has a wide-ranging impact. The goal of IPM is to keep insects, diseases, and weeds at tolerable levels using the least toxic methods available. Techniques include planting pest-resistant cultivars, following appropriate lawn-care practices, inspecting regularly for problems, encouraging beneficial insects, and when necessary, spot-treating affected areas.

Let's face it: bugs are here to stay. Most of them are actually desirable and serve important functions in biological processes such as decomposition. Others are considered beneficial because their diet includes the insects chomping on your grass. Studies have shown that predators such as ants and ground beetles are able to remove up to 74 percent of Japanese beetle eggs and up to 53 percent of fall armyworm pupae from pesticide-free plots within 48 hours. Before reaching for the insecticide, wait a while to give these natural enemies of pests a

chance to bring your problem under control. Read on to learn more about the numerous insects that call your yard home, as well as how you can keep the upper hand.

● ●

Did You Know? *The Environmental Protection Agency estimates that U.S. homeowners apply about 70 million pounds of pesticides to their lawns each year.*

NOT JUST FOR BIRDS

Smart TIP

Those birds reveling in the backyard dust know what they're doing. Finely ground particles in such dust baths damage the exoskeletons of bothersome insects. Diatomaceous earth, a dust used to control caterpillars, works on the same principle. Composed of fossilized remains of single-celled plants called diatoms, these ancient deposits are quarried and then processed to form a dust. People and animals are not bothered by this material, but many soft-bodied insects are because it destroys either their protective outer layer or gut. Used primarily for garden pests, it will also help control aphids and ants in the lawn. If you plan to use diatomaceous earth to control pests, be sure to buy the type meant for horticultural use, not the type for use in swimming pool filters.

Visible Clues to Insects

Knowing your local pests and their life cycles is the key to determining whether lawn damage is due to insects. The rest is a matter of keeping your eyes open. Most insects are large enough to be visible, so don't wait for your grass to start dying to find out there's a problem.

The presence of sod webworms may become apparent one evening, when you see their adult form, a buff-colored moth, zigzagging across the lawn. And consider those June beetles banging against the screens at night or the Japanese beetles eating your roses—they should alert you to the fact that their larvae may be damaging your grass roots. Another clue to the presence of underground insects is small upturned areas where skunks dig by night and birds congregate by day.

Looking closely at the lawn, using a magnifying glass when necessary, will enable you to see signs of chewing or the tiny light spots indicative of sucking insects. You may also see the tunnel openings of mole crickets or the actual culprits.

Becoming an insect sleuth isn't difficult, and your persistence will pay off. The byword here is *vigilance*—making a habit of closely observing your turf. And remember, just a few bugs are nothing to worry about. You only need to take action when the population approaches damaging levels. The following list is divided into insects causing damage aboveground and those that work underground.

Aboveground Pests

Chinch bugs

The premier pest on St. Augustinegrass lawns, chinch bugs are found on other grasses as well, in all but the coldest cli-

Earthworms Are More Than Fish Bait

Abundant in moist, heavy soils, earthworms are a natural component of healthy lawns. Their diet of dirt, organic matter, and plant litter is excreted in the form of a rich digestive by-product called castings. These small, hardened piles can be found scattered across the ground. While initially they can be felt underfoot, castings will eventually break down, providing your lawn with a dose of natural fertilizer. Worm castings are sold commercially for this very purpose.

In addition to providing nutrients for plants, earthworms aid in thatch decomposition. They also improve soil aeration and increase water penetration through their extensive burrowing.

EARTHWORMS ARE A SURE SIGN OF EXCELLENT SOIL CONDITIONS. THEIR CASTINGS ARE A NATURAL FERTILIZER.

mates. Black, winged, and ⅕ inch long, they live in the thatch layer where eggs are laid at the root line. Most damaging are the tiny red nymphs, which thrive on sap sucked from grass stems.

Look for: Yellow patches that don't improve with watering, starting in June, in hot, dry, sunny lawn areas. Look under the grass canopy to see nymphs and adults. An alternative is to use the water flotation test. (See "Testing for Insects," page 159.) If you see 20 to 25 bugs over five minutes, you need to take action.

Management: Maintain minimum fertilization; irrigate regularly; keep thatch low; and raise mowing height. Encourage beneficial big-eyed bugs, and use endopyhte-enhanced, resistant grass cultivars. For St. Augustinegrass, 'Floralawn' and 'Floratam' are resistant varieties; 'Floratine' is considered tolerant to chinch bugs. If cultivars don't cure the problem, consider spot treatment with insecticidal soap or pyrethrin.

Sod webworms

Nighttime feeders that usually aren't noticed until damage is ob-

Watch What You Step On

It pays to know what insects look like throughout their life cycle, because they change form as they grow in a process called metamorphosis. Born with rigid or semirigid outer skins, insects would have a difficult time growing if they weren't able to shed this covering as they outgrew it. Some insects—such as beetles, lacewings, and moths—start life as larvae and evolve to an intermediate stage at which they are called pupae. After more molting, they assume their adult form, which looks completely different from the earlier stages. Such a total transformation is called a complete metamorphosis.

Most people are familiar with the caterpillar-to-butterfly cycle, but many people are not aware of what lady beetles and lacewings look like in infancy. During this larval stage, these and some other beneficial insects have an especially voracious appetite for pests. Unfortunately for these helpful bugs, they are so ugly as larvae and so unlike their familiar adult forms that unknowing gardeners often squash them.

Other insects do not experience the same degree of transformation; instead they go through a gradual metamorphosis. These insects are called nymphs in their immature stage, when they look like smaller versions of their adult forms. Mantids and aphids are examples of such insects.

LADY BEETLES BEGIN LIFE LOOKING LIKE THIS.

IN ITS LARVAL STAGE, IT LOOKS ANYTHING BUT CUTE.

IN ITS PUPAL STAGE, THE LADYBUG FINALLY BEGINS TO TAKE ITS ADULT SHAPE.

vious, these small, green, spotted caterpillars feed on grass roots, crowns, and leaves. The adult form, a small, whitish gray to brown moth, can be seen in the evening taking short, jerky flights across the lawn.

Look for: Irregular brown patches of short or uneven turf in early spring, especially in hot, dry areas. On close inspection, you may see silken grass tunnels used for daytime shelter and green waste pellets in the thatch. To check the population level, use a soap drench over affected areas; 15 webworms per square yard requires action.

Management: Damage can be outgrown with an extra dose of fertilizer in the spring and increased irrigation. Thatch should be minimized and ground beetles encouraged. *Bacillus thuringiensis* (BT) is effective on young larvae, and *Steinernema* nematodes are a useful biological control. Endophyte-enhanced perennial ryegrasses, tall fescues, and fine fescues are recommended resistant turfs that will thwart hungry webworms.

Fall armyworms

At 1½ to 2 inches, these striped, brownish-green nighttime feeders are twice as long as webworms. Basically a southern insect, they move north either as spring-migrating moths or as caterpillar armies seeking food in summer and fall.

Look for: Chewed, bare, circular areas, similar to the damage of webworms, except that armyworms don't make tunnels. With large infestations, damage can accumulate quickly.

Management: Use of BT spray, some botanical insecticides (such as natural pyrethrum), and parasitic nematodes (such as *Steinernema carpocapsae*) will help. Encourage predators such as braconid wasps, ground beetles, and birds. Maintain optimal conditions to encourage new growth.

• •

Did You Know? *Earthworms loosen and aerate the soil, and they feed the grass with their castings. Ten earthworms per 10 square feet of soil is generally considered a good number.*

Leafhoppers

These tiny, wedge-shaped, green, yellow, or brown flying bugs suck sap from leaves while injecting toxins into the grass. Lawn damage is usually slight.

Look for: Mottled whitish patches with leaves browned along the edge and curled at the tips. When disturbed, leafhoppers will hop away or, if adults, fly.

Management: Maintain lawn vigor through regular cultural practices. Encourage lacewings and ladybugs. Insecticidal soap or botanical insecticides may be used for severe infestations.

Green aphids

These tiny pear-shaped insects (sometimes called greenbugs) feed on the juices of grass blades while injecting a salivary toxin. They have been causing se-

rious damage to Kentucky bluegrass lawns in some Midwestern states since the mid-1970s.

Look for: Yellowing of turf, frequently in sunny locations but sometimes extending out from the base of shade tree trunks. Close inspection will reveal the aphids. The use of a 10x hand lens is helpful for identifying insects. Hand lenses are available in different powers at botanical garden gift shops and through gardening catalogue companies.

Management: A good old-fashioned hosing down will discourage aphids from returning. Natural predators such as lady beetles, lacewings, big-eyed bugs, ground beetles, and parasitic wasps should be encouraged. For large infestations, use insecticidal soap. Botanical insecticides may be warranted.

Underground Pests

White grubs

These root-eating larvae of the scarab beetle family include Japanese beetles, June bugs, rose chafers, and the black turfgrass ataenius. Grub size and characteristics vary, but generally grubs are plump, whitish gray, and C-shaped with brown heads, and they have three pairs of legs. Watching in summer for adult Japanese beetles, which are metallic green with copper wings, or June bugs, which are reddish brown nocturnal fliers, will help with identification.

Look for: Wilted, bluish-gray grass that initially looks like drought damage in late spring and then becomes dried and browned-out turf later in the season. With the roots eaten, the turf will roll back when pulled on. Once soil heats up to 60°F in spring, grubs may be observed in the top few inches of dirt. Unless the grass is already in poor condition, control is usually not necessary until you have 10 to 15 grubs per square foot.

Management: Before using milky spore disease to combat Japanese beetle grubs, check with your Cooperative Extension Service to see if the spore is effective in your area. Studies indicate that milky spore, especially in colder climates, is less effective than previously thought.

Because these beetles prefer moist soil for laying eggs, one tactic is to water deeply but infrequently during the summer. White grubs are also susceptible to parasitic nematodes such as *Steinernema car-*

Aboveground Munchers

The adult chinch bug, ABOVE, IS THE SCOURGE OF SOUTHERN GRASSES. THE CHINCH BUG NYMPH, LEFT, SUCKS ON SAP FROM GRASS STEMS, CAUSING THEM TO WITHER.

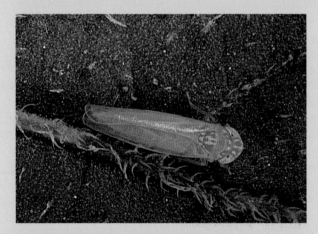

Leafhopper POPULATIONS CAN BE KEPT IN CHECK WITH LADYBUGS AND OTHER BENEFICIAL INSECTS.

The sod webworm, A SPOTTED CATERPILLAR, FEEDS ON GRASS AND EVENTUALLY BECOMES A MOTH.

The fall armyworm DOES ITS DAMAGE AT NIGHT. PARASITIC NEMATODES WILL HELP KEEP IT IN CHECK.

Green aphids (ALSO CALLED GREENBUGS), PREVALENT IN THE MIDWEST, WILL CAUSE TURF TO TURN YELLOW.

Underground Munchers

If Japanese beetles ARE EATING YOUR SHRUBS OR TREES, LEFT, THEIR LARVAE ARE PROBABLY EATING YOUR GRASS ROOTS, ABOVE.

A mole cricket, ABOVE, IS ALSO A ROOT FEEDER. IT PREFERS LIGHT, SANDY SOILS. IT LEAVES BROWN, DRY PATCHES OF TURF IN ITS WAKE, LEFT.

pocapsae. If damage warrants reseeding, turning over the soil and either hand-picking the grubs or leaving them exposed for birds may serve as a short-term alternative.

Billbugs

The C-shaped, small white larvae of this weevil cause more damage than the adult. Found more commonly in northern states, billbugs prefer Kentucky bluegrass, feeding on stems, crowns, and eventually roots.

Look for: Irregular dry patches the color of whitish straw that develop by midsummer. When affected grass is tugged, it breaks off at the root line, exposing hollowed-out stems packed with sawdust-like material. Unlike its condition after grub damage, the turf will not feel spongy. You may note some of the legless larvae underground.

Management: Nematodes are showing promise for this difficult-to-control bug. Use of resistant bluegrass varieties, such as 'Park', 'Arista', 'NuDwarf', and 'Delta', or endophyte-enhanced ryegrass and fescues, is recommended. Rotenone, a botanical insecticide, may be used for spot treatment.

Mole crickets

These large crickets with short, stout forelegs feed on grass roots and tunnel through underground root zones. They are especially damaging pests in the light, sandy soils of the southern and Gulf plains. They prefer bahiagrass but feed on whatever grass is available.

Look for: Small tunnel openings and spongy earth along with browned, dry patches of turf. Use a soap drench and observe for three minutes. (See "Testing for Insects," right.) Finding two to four crickets per 4 square feet is significant.

Management: Follow practices to encourage deep roots and to keep thatch low. Use low-nitrogen fertilizer to avoid developing overly succulent growth, and mow high. Research done at the University of Florida has shown promising results using a parasitic nematode, *Steinernema scaperisci*. Also, ground beetles are a beneficial predator.

So You've Got Bugs

Having done your homework and identified the particular insects damaging your lawn, you can decide what, if anything, to do about them. There are guidelines for how many insects in a given area constitute a threat. The tricky part is that vigorous lawns can withstand greater numbers of pests than those under stress. Thus a healthy lawn might not show signs of injury in the spring despite having a high number of Japanese beetle grubs per square foot. But the same lawn, when semidormant in late summer, might develop significant problems with just 6 to 10 grubs per square foot. Before making treatment decisions, consider how healthy your lawn is to start with, where the insect is in its life cycle, and how much damage you can tolerate.

If the population numbers and extent of grass injury warrant action, your first step might be to physically remove as many bugs as possible. (See

Testing for Insects

In addition to the time-honored method of parting the grass and looking around, the following techniques will expose the damaging insects in your lawn.

Soap Drench. Useful for flushing out sod webworms, armyworms, mole crickets, and caterpillars. Mix 5 to 6 tablespoons of dish-washing liquid in a 2-gallon sprinkling can full of water, and then drench 4 square feet of lawn with the solution. Observe the area for three minutes, counting the number of bugs that emerge.

Water Flotation Test. Used for chinch bugs. Cut both ends off of a 2- to 3-pound coffee can, and push it 2 or 3 inches into the soil at the margin of a yellowed area of grass. Fill the can with water, and maintain its level above the grass surface for five minutes as you watch for chinch bugs to float to the top.

Sod Lift. Used for grubs, billbugs, and rose chafer larvae. Using a spade, cut three sides of a 1-foot-square piece of sod about 2 inches deep, and lay back the sod flap. Check grass roots to see if they are chewed off, and sift through the top several inches of soil to count larvae. Replace the sod and water well.

BY LIFTING A SECTION OF SOD ONCE PER SEASON, YOU'LL GET A GOOD LOOK AT WHAT'S FEEDING ON YOUR LAWN.

"Mechanical Bug Removal," below.) Next, reduce thatch levels and compaction where they are problems. You should also consider whether your lawn needs some extra TLC to help it recover more quickly. Don't cut the grass too short or add water stress to its list of woes!

If despite your best efforts, pest populations aren't restrained through the more benign efforts of cultivation, grass selection, and competition from beneficial insects, you may need to use biological insecticides, botanical insecticides, or insecticidal soaps. These have the environmental advantage of rapidly breaking down when exposed to sunlight, heat, and water, so they don't persist on vegetation or in the soil. They are considered less toxic to humans than synthetic products, but they can still upset the ecological balance in your yard and cause more harm than good if used improperly. Be sure to read labels and follow directions carefully, including the use of protective masks and clothing—some of these substances are severe irritants. When using sprays, avoid the middle of the day when they will be less effective, and time applications to take advantage of pest life cycles.

Biological Insecticides

The advantage of using biological or microbial insecticides is that they are only harmful to specifically targeted pests. They are not injurious to wildlife, humans, or other soil microbes or insects. Furthermore, they don't leave toxic residues behind to worry about. They do come with some cautions, though. The mold spores, bacterial spores, and other living organisms that make up these products can produce allergic reactions in some people. Handle them with care; wear protective clothing; avoid inhaling them or rubbing them on your skin; and follow all provided directions.

Bacillus thuringiensis (BT) is composed of a crystalline protein produced by the spores of a soil bacterium. When ingested by targeted pests, it destroys their gut lining, stopping their feeding and killing them. Insect-specific strains are sold as dusts, emulsions, and wettable powder. BT is highly selective and viable for only a few days after application. Apply in late afternoon for the best results.

Bacillus popilliae, or milky spore disease, has been the chief biological agent for Japanese beetle control. Its efficacy is now in question, however, especially in northern soils. Check with your Cooperative Extension Service for local recommendations. Only one or two applications of milky spore disease are needed because, once it kills the grubs, fungal endospores are released into the soil to await their next host. However, this product is not effective for other kinds of white grubs.

Steinernematidae and Heterorhabditidae are predatory nematodes. These microscopic, worm-like parasites live in moist soil and attack the larvae of lawn pests, such as billbugs, sod webworms, and white grubs. Beneficial nematodes are not harmful to plants, and different strains are sold to target specific pests. The use of predatory nematodes is a quickly growing area of horticultural research that shows much promise.

Your choice of nematode should be based on the target pest's habitat. For moist-soil and deeper-dwelling pests (3 to 6 inches), heterorhabditid nematodes are the way to go. *Steinernema carpocapsae* is more effective on surface feeders because of its better mobility.

Remember that nematodes are living organisms. They need moisture to keep them from drying out and to aid in their movement, so be sure to irrigate release areas before and

Mechanical Bug Removal

When pests are visible and large enough, removing them via the "pick and squash" method is an option for the nonsqueamish. Try the following on insects you can't see.

For chinch bugs, prepare a soap drench with 2 tablespoons of dish-washing liquid and 2 gallons of water in a watering can. Thoroughly water an off-color patch of lawn, and then cover it with a flannel sheet. Wait 15 minutes; then scrape clinging bugs off the sheet and into a garbage bag.

For sod webworms, drench the target areas with a soap solution, and watch for the worms to climb up from the thatch layer. Rake them up and dispose of them in the garbage or in water. When mechanical controls are not feasible, consider using the biological controls, botanical (plant-derived) insecticides, or insecticidal soaps described in this chapter.

Nematodes

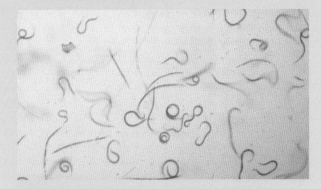

PREDATORY NEMATODES ATTACK LAWN PESTS SUCH AS BILLBUGS, SOD WEBWORMS, AND WHITE GRUBS.

NEMATODES ARE PARASITES THAT CAN KILL HOSTS, SUCH AS THIS GRUB, WITHIN 48 HRS. SOME NEMATODES ATTACK SURFACE PESTS; OTHERS ATTACK SOIL-DWELLING PESTS. CHOOSE THE CORRECT TYPE FOR YOUR PEST.

NEMATODES ARRIVE BY MAIL IN A SPONGE, ABOVE. TO APPLY, PLACE THE SPONGE IN A CONTAINER OF COLD WATER AND WRING IT SEVERAL TIMES TO RELEASE THE NEMATODES. APPLY WITH A WATERING CAN OR SPRAYER.

after application. It's best to release nematodes at night, during warm weather, and when humidity is high and the soil temperature is 55° to 90°F. Nematodes are available from garden suppliers specializing in organic gardening products.

Botanical Insecticides

Botanical insecticides are not targeted to specific pests, and they often kill beneficial insects as well. They are best used only as a last resort, when more direct methods fail. Although they do not persist long in the environment, botanical insecticides can be quite toxic when applied, so handle them with care and always follow package directions, including wearing protective clothing.

Pyrethrins are made from extracts of pyrethrum flowers, two species of chrysanthemum. Known for

their ability to "knock down" flying insects, pyrethrins are frequently combined with synergists, such as piperonyl butoxide, which increases the pyrethrins' toxicity and length of residual action. Used against aphids, armyworms, beetles, caterpillars, leafhoppers, and other pests, pyrethrins are also toxic to fish and some beneficial insects.

Rotenone, one of the oldest botanical insecticides, is extracted from the roots of the Asian plant *Derris elliptica.* This slow-acting general insecticide is highly toxic to fish and moderately so for mammals. It's also very irritating to the respiratory tract.

Sabadilla, one of the least toxic botanical insecticides, is made from the seeds of the Venezuelan plant Sabadilla (*Schoenocaulon officinale*). Used as a dust or spray to kill grasshoppers, armyworms, webworms, aphids, and chinch bugs, this insecticide breaks down rapidly in sunlight. Sabadilla is highly irritating to the respiratory tract and eyes.

Neem is derived from an oil extracted from the Indian Neem tree. It's effective on multiple fronts—repelling insects, stopping them from feeding, inhibiting molting, and suppressing growth, Neem affects leaf-chewing beetles, caterpillars, and other insects that are in the process of going through metamorphosis. It has low toxicity for mammals, including humans.

Insecticidal Soaps

Insecticidal soaps are made from the potassium salts of fatty acids. On direct contact with susceptible insects, these acids disrupt the structure and permeability of their cell membranes, causing desiccation and death. Most effective on soft-bodied insects, including beneficials, these soaps have a minimum impact on ladybug larvae and parasitic wasps. Aside

from causing mild eye and skin irritation, they have low mammalian toxicity. They are biodegradable. Once they dry, however, they are no longer effective.

Beneficial Insects

Creating an environment hostile to pests includes enlisting the help of beneficials. These insects keep undesirable pest populations in check through their feeding, as either predators or parasites. Both the adult and immature stages of predators actively search out and consume their prey. Parasites help by depositing their eggs in or on the host prey. When they hatch, the host becomes their food source.

What can you do to encourage helpful insects? Well, there's nothing like a nontoxic environment, a bit of nectar, a sip of water, and a protected spot to keep beneficials from wandering. Here's how to make your yard attractive to beneficials by looking after their basic needs.

Beneficial Insects

LADY BEETLE

GROUND BEETLE

PRAYING MANTID

LACEWING

LARVAL LACEWING

BIG-EYED BUG

First, avoid using pesticides. You don't want to harm the good guys, and you don't want to starve them by poisoning their favorite insect food sources. Second, beneficial insects are more likely to remain in your yard if you provide their favorite pollen and nectar sources. Common herbs such as fennel, dill, spearmint, caraway, and coriander, and tansy would be a good start. While you're at it, plant a border that includes some wildflowers, such as yarrow and Queen Anne's lace, along with nasturtiums and other flowering plants, which will provide a succession of blooms. (See "A Garden for Beneficials," page 164.)

Water is also important and can be

SPINED SOLDIER BUG

BRACONID WASP ON A CATERPILLAR

supplied by sinking a few shallow pans with small rocks in them into the soil. They will fill from rain or watering. Finally, places to shelter and overwinter can be provided by the addition of shrubs, vines, or small evergreens. If these sheltering plants include berry-bearing plants such as chokeberry, bayberry, sumacs, and viburnums, the fruits will attract grub-eating birds for additional pest control. The following are some insects that feed on lawn pests.

Lady beetles, also known as ladybugs, are perhaps the most widely recognized beneficial insects. As adults, and especially in the larval form, ladybugs feed on aphids and other small, soft-bodied insect pests. Adults have short legs and antennae, are ¼ inch or smaller, oval, brightly colored, and often spotted. Their ravenous larvae resemble tiny alligators with flat, gray bodies tapering to the tail, with red or orange spots.

Ground beetles, known as "caterpillar hunters," are valuable nocturnal predators with a taste for beetle grubs, caterpillars, armyworms, and cutworms. These fast-moving creatures, ¾ to 1 inch long with flattened blue, black, or brown bodies, spend their days hiding under stones and garden debris. Larvae are long, dark, and tapered, with segmented bodies.

Mantids are large green or brownish insects up to 4 inches long. Called "praying mantids" or "praying mantis" after the position in which they hold their front legs, they are voracious predators who even eat their own young. While still considered beneficial, they are nonselective in choosing their prey and may consume helpful insects, including each other, as well as pests.

Lacewings are green to the east of the Rocky Mountains and brown to the west. These delicate ½- to ¾-inch-long insects, when at rest, hold their clear and highly veined wings up like a tent. Their larvae are called "aphid lions," but they're not averse to eating other pests, such as caterpillar eggs or leafhopper nymphs.

Big-eyed bugs are especially helpful where chinch bugs are a problem. This bulging-eyed, ⅛- to ¼-inch-long black or gray insect also eats leafhoppers, aphids, and caterpillars. Unlike most insect predators, the bugs in this family (*Lygaeidae Geocoris* species) have been known to take an occasional bite or two from plants.

Spined soldier bugs are beneficials but are often mistaken for their stinkbug cousins, which are pests. This ½-inch-long lover of caterpillars, grubs, and fall armyworms has a shield-shaped body and is differentiated from stinkbugs by pointed shoulders and a black mark on the wing membrane.

Braconid wasps are slender ⅒- to ½-inch parasites that deposit eggs either inside of the host prey or in pupal cocoons on or near a dead host insect. In this way, a small species of braconid wasps parasitizes aphids, and a larger species parasitizes a wide variety of beetles, caterpillars, and other insects.

A Garden for Beneficials

Gardens designed to encourage high beneficial insect populations should incorporate a variety of flowering plants rich in nectar and pollen. Choose cultivars with easily accessible pollen that is found in plants that have just a single layer of petals or a tubular flower form. Common herbs, wildflowers, and scented plants are all attractive to beneficial insects. Remember that come fall the dead foliage will continue to be an important habitat for beneficials over the winter, so don't clear it out.

Spring

Columbine (Aquilegia *species*)
Perennial blooming in early spring.

Rosemary (Rosmarinus officinalis)
Perennial herb blooming in early spring.

Violet (Viola *species*)
Perennial blooming in early spring.

Queen Anne's lace (Daucus carota)
Biennial blooming spring through summer.

Stonecrop (Sedum *species*)
Perennial blooming spring through summer.

Blue salvia (Salvia farinacea)
Annual blooming late spring through summer.

Dill (Anethum graveolens)
Annual herb blooming late spring through summer.

Lemon balm (Melissa officinalis)
Perennial herb blooming late spring through summer.

Tickseed (Coreopsis *species*)
Perennial blooming late spring through summer.

Thyme (Thymus *species*)
Perennial herb blooming late spring through summer

Summer

Coriander (Coriandrum sativum)

Plants That Attract Beneficials

CORIANDER (*CORIANDRUM SATIVUM*)

JOHNNY JUMP UP (*VIOLA CORNUTA*)

MOSSY STONECROP WALLPEPPER (*SEDUM* SPECIES)

Annual herb blooming in early summer.

Fennel (**Foeniculum vulgare**)
Biennial herb blooming in summer.

Lavender (**Lavandula** *species*)
Perennial herb blooming in summer.

Parsley (**Petroselinum crispum**)
Biennial blooming in summer.

Sage (**Salvia officinalis**)
Perennial herb blooming in summer.

Tansy (**Tanacetum vulgare**)
Perennial herb blooming in summer.

Summer Into Fall

Marigold (**Tagetes** *species*)
Annual blooming early summer into late fall.

Bee balm (**Monarda didyma**)
Perennial blooming summer into fall.

Purple coneflower (**Echinacea purpurea**)
Perennial blooming summer into fall.

Cosmos (**Cosmos bipinnatus**)
Annual blooming summer into fall.

Cumin (**Cuminum cyminum**)
Annual herb blooming summer into fall.

Goldenrod (**Solidago** *species*)
Perennial blooming summer into fall.

Mint (**Mentha** *species*)
Perennial herb blooming summer into fall.

Joe-Pye weed (**Eupatorium** *species*)
Perennial blooming summer into fall.

Yarrow (**Achillea** *species*)
Perennial blooming summer into fall.

Aster (**Aster** *species*)
Perennial blooming late summer into late fall.

Chrysanthemum (**Chrysanthemum** *species*)
Perennial blooming summer into late fall.

Nasturtium (**Tropaeolum** *species*)
Annual blooming summer into late fall.

COSMOS (*COSMOS BIPINNATUS*)

NASTURTIUMS (*TROPAEOLUM* SPECIES)

HORSEMINT (*MENTHA LONGFOLIA*)

HEAVY-DUTY LATEX GLOVES THAT EXTEND TO THE FORE-ARM AND FIT SNUGLY AROUND THE WRIST OFFER THE BEST PROTECTION WHEN APPLYING HERBICIDES AND PESTICIDES.

Safe Pesticide Use

- *Use the least toxic, most target-specific chemical.*
- *Purchase the smallest amount needed to do the job.*
- *Don't mix more spray than you need—and stick to target areas only.*
- *Read the label carefully, and follow all recommendations precisely.*
- *Wear protective clothing and gear as directed.*
- *Wear gloves when using a sprayer, and wash well afterward.*
- *Don't use pesticides if rain is forecast or if it's windy.*
- *Launder pesticide-contaminated clothing separately.*
- *Keep leftover pesticides away from children*
- *Keep leftover chemicals in their original containers.*
- *Contact the National Pesticide Information Center (800-858-7378, npic.orst.edu) for more information.*

Synthetic Toxins: A Last Resort

In its consumer booklet *Citizen's Guide to Pest Control and Pesticide Safety*, the EPA states that healthy lawns will have some weeds and insect pests as well as beneficial insects and earthworms. The guide notes that following a preventative health-care program for your lawn should enable you to avoid most pesticide use.

It's important to think of turf diseases and insect damage as symptoms of a breakdown in your lawn's ecosystem rather than as problems to attack with toxins. When problems occur, your first step should be diagnosis, followed by an adjustment of your cultural practices to alleviate the causes. If treatment becomes necessary, start with mechanical and biological controls. Synthetic chemical products should be a last resort. Use of synthetics will provide only temporary relief, and unlike botanical toxins, many synthetics remain potent in the environment long after their application. They can contaminate ground water and kill off needed soil microorganisms and beneficial insects.

If you feel that your lawn pest problem is so serious that it warrants the use of synthetic chemicals, try to use the least toxic products you can and those that break down relatively quickly. Also check with your Cooperative Extension Service for local recommendations.

Taking Cover

Whether you're using insecticides and herbicides derived from botanical, biological, or synthetic materials, take all basic precautions, including the use of goggles, disposable dust masks (for pesticide dusts), and tight-fitting respirators when using liquid sprays. Respirators contain activated charcoal cartridges that filter pesticide vapors from the air. Make sure it's approved by the National Institute of Occupational Safety and Health (NIOSH).

Read product labels thoroughly, and apply these products with great care. Wear a hat, hood, or scarf to completely cover your scalp and to overhang your face. Wear a long–sleeved shirt, pants, and socks made of tightly woven material (all cotton). Do not leave skin exposed! Gloves and footwear should be waterproof. If your clothing becomes wet with the pesticide, remove it immediately. Shower directly after using these products and before changing into uncontaminated clothes.

Be sure to rinse off your waterproof gear and pesticide applicator using plenty of clean water before removing your protective apparel. Avoid handling the outside of the contaminated clothing; use gloves if necessary. If the clothing will not be laundered immediately, place the clothing in a sealable plastic bag. Wash these garments separately from your regular laundry. Presoak them in a presoaking product; then wash them on the highest temperature setting for a full cycle with detergent. If the clothing has any residual pesticide odor after the rinse cycle, repeat the washing procedure until the odor is gone. Air-dry the wet clothes on a line; then wash the washing machine by running it through the wash cycle with detergent but without clothes. Or simply throw the clothes away.

Moles in the Lawn

Insects aren't the only pests to bother lawns. Some four-footed varmints—moles—may also take up residence. You might first become aware that these small creatures are in your lawn when you nearly trip stepping into the soft earth of a tunnel. Moles create these passageways as they burrow underground in their almost constant search for food. Moles eat an estimated 40 pounds of insects a year and tunnel day and night looking for food. The dirt pushed up in this effort leaves a network of low ridges across the landscape and an occasional pile of surplus dirt—a molehill.

Moles are difficult to get rid of. A skilled mole-hunting dog or cat can keep a mole population down. But trapping is considered the most effective means of eliminating moles. Designed to kill moles in their tunnels, traps should be placed in main activity tunnels, not in the shallow, temporary branches. Main tunnels run underground at a depth of 1 to 5 inches. Because moles can't hibernate, winter tunnels can be more than 24 inches deep.

Where tunneling is visible, look for straight runs with branches coming off of them. Test for tunnels by caving in straight sections with your feet; then recheck later to see if the tunnels have been rebuilt. Rebuilding indicates main thoroughfares.

You can also find main tunnels by using a rod to probe the ground around molehills. You will feel a sudden give when the rod pierces a tunnel. There are a number of traps on the market. Your choice will depend on the type of moles in your area.

About Moles

MOLES BUILD NEAR-SURFACE TUNNELS, ABOVE, AS WELL AS DEEPER TUNNELS. MICE USE THE TUNNELS TO FEED ON ROOTS AND BULBS, LEAVING MOLES TO TAKE THE BLAME. MOLES DON'T EAT ROOTS OR BULBS BUT MAY DISPLACE THEM, CAUSING THEM TO DRY OUT AND DIE. MOLES FEED MAINLY ON EARTHWORMS BUT ALSO EAT GRUBS AND OTHER INSECTS.

RESOURCE GUIDE

The following list of manufacturers and associations is meant to be a general guide to additional industry and product-related sources. It is not intended as a listing of products and manufacturers represented by the photographs in this book.

Beyond Pesticides
701 East St. SE, Ste. 200
Washington, DC 20003
202-543-5450
www.beyondpesticides.org
A nonprofit organization that provides information on pesticides and promotes the reduction of unnecessary pesticide use.

Bio-Integral Resource Center (BIRC)
P.O. Box 7414
Berkeley, CA 94707
510-524-2567
www.birc.org
A nonprofit organization that offers insight in the development and communication of least-toxic, sustainable, and environmentally sound Integrated Pest Management (IPM) methods.

Cooperative State Research, Education, and Extension Service (CSREES)
U.S. Department of Agriculture
Waterfront Centre
800 Ninth St. SW
Washington, DC 20024
202-720-7441
www.csrees.usda.gov/
An agency that helps fund—at the state and local levels—research, education, and extension programs in order to advance knowledge for agriculture, the environment, human health, and well-being.

Gardens Alive!
5100 Schenley Pl.
Lawrenceburg, IN 47025
513-354-1482
www.gardensalive.com

A mail-order company that offers environmentally responsible products for lawns and gardens.

Guelph Turfgrass Institute
328 Victoria Rd. South, R.R. #2
Guelph, ON, Canada N1H 6H8
519-767-5009
www.uoguelph.ca/GTI/
Center for research, extension, and professional development in areas such as pesticide use, evaluation of grass species, and seeding methods.

The Lawn Institute
2 East Main St.
East Dundee, IL 60018
800-405-8873
www.lawninstitute.com
A nonprofit corporation that assists in and encourages the improvement of lawns and sports turf through research and education.

National Turfgrass Evaluation Program (NTEP)
Beltsville Agricultural Research Center West
10300 Baltimore Ave.
Bldg. 003, Rm. 218
Beltsville, MD 20705
301-504-5125
www.ntep.org
Tests, evaluates, and identifies turfgrass species.

Natural Insect Control (NIC)
3737 Netherby Rd.
Stevensville, ON, Canada L0S 1S0
905-382-2904
www.natural-insect-control.com
Offers organic fertilizers and environmentally friendly pest-control products.

Northwest Coalition for Alternatives to Pesticides (NCAP)
P.O. Box 1393
Eugene, OR 97440
541-344-5044
www.pesticide.org
An advocacy group that provides information on pesticides and offers alternatives to their use.

Peaceful Valley Farm & Garden Supply
P.O. Box 2209
Grass Valley, CA 95945
530-272-4769
www.groworganic.com
Offers tools and supplies for organic farming and gardening, including in-ground irrigation supplies, pest-control products, and soil test kits.

Rachel Carson Council, Inc.
P.O. Box 10779
Silver Spring, MD 20914
301-593-7507
www.rachelcarsoncouncil.com
A nonprofit organization focused on collecting and providing information on chemical pesticides and providing alternative methods of pest control.

The Scotts Miracle-Gro Company
14111 Scottslawn Rd.
Marysville, OH 43041
888-270-3714
www.scotts.com
Provides lawn and garden products, including lawn fertilizer, weed and insect control, grass seeds, soils, mulches, plant food, and spreaders.

The Toro Company
8111 Lyndale Ave. South
Bloomington, MN 55420
888-384-9939
www.toro.com
Manufactures outdoor power equipment, including mowers, lawn tractors, zero-turn-radius mowers, and irrigation products.

Woodstream Corporation
P.O. Box 327
Lititz, PA 17543
800-800-1819
www.woodstream.com
Manufactures a variety of natural and organic Safer® Brand products for lawn care, gardening, and pest control.

GLOSSARY

Acid soil Soil with a pH measure below 7. Most soils in the eastern third of the United States and Canada and along the West Coast are naturally acidic. Also called sour soil.

Aeration Introduction of air to compacted soil by mechanically removing plugs of topsoil. Aeration helps oxygen, water, fertilizer, and organic matter to reach roots. Also called core cultivation or aerifying.

Alkaline soil Soil with a pH measure above 7. Many central and western states have alkaline soils. Also called sweet soil.

Amendments Organic or mineral materials, such as peat moss, compost, or perlite, that are used to improve the soil.

Annual A plant that germinates, grows, flowers, produces seeds, and dies in the course of a single growing season. Annual grasses are sometimes used as nurse crops to protect slower-growing seed, or to overseed warm-season grasses during their dormancy.

Automated home sprinkler system A method for watering lawn and plantings via underground pipes and sprinklers. A controller, when set to run, directs water to one station (valve) at a time for a specified amount of time. Afterward, it closes the valve and opens the next valve. Each station sends water to one zone, which typically consists of a group of sprinklers.

Automatic valves Electrically operated valves that turn water on and off at signals from the controller. They are typically buried in valve boxes, several valves to a box.

Cool-season grasses Grasses that thrive in northern areas, including Canada, and in high elevations in the South.

Compost Humus made by decomposing vegetative matter in a compost bin or pile.

Crown The part of a plant where the roots and stem meet, usually at soil level.

Cultivar A cultivated variety of a plant, often bred for a desirable trait, such as pest- or disease-resistance.

Drainage The movement of water through the soil. With good drainage, water disappears from a planting hole in less than a few hours. If water remains standing overnight, drainage is poor.

Drip irrigation A low-pressure system for irrigating gardens, shrubs, and lawns. Water is released slowly over longer periods of time by emitters or sprayers, and it is applied as close to plant roots as possible. Typically used

Brick edging on sand and gravel

on the surface or just under the mulch of a garden bed, drip irrigation can be used underground to irrigate lawns.

Edging A shallow trench or physical barrier of metal, wood, brick, or synthetic material used to define the border between lawn turf and another area, such as paving or a flower bed.

Endophytes Fungi that live in some grasses (called endophytic), making them harmful or deadly to a variety of aboveground grass-eating insects.

Exposure The intensity, duration, and variation in sun, wind, and temperature that characterize any particular lawn or planting site.

Frost heave, frost heaving A disturbance or uplift of soil, pavement, or plants caused by moisture in the soil freezing and expanding.

Full shade A site that receives no direct sun during the growing season.

Full sun A site that receives at least eight hours of direct sun each day during the growing season.

Grade The degree and direction of slope on an area of ground.

Ground cover A plant, such as ivy, liriope, or juniper, used to cover the soil and form a continuous low mass of foliage. Often used as a substitute for turfgrass.

Hardiness A plant's ability to survive the winter without protection from the cold.

Hardiness zone A region where the coldest temperature in an average winter falls within a certain range, such as between 0° and –10°F.

Heat zone A region determined by the average annual number of days its temperatures climb above 86°F.

Herbicide A chemical used to kill plants. Preemergent herbicides are used to kill weed seeds as they sprout and thus to prevent weed growth. Post-emergent herbicides kill plants that are already growing.

Humus Thoroughly decayed organic matter. Added to lawns, it will increase a soil's water-holding capacity, improve aeration, and support beneficial microbial life in the soil.

Invasive A plant that spreads quickly, usually by runners, and mixes with or dominates adjacent plantings.

Landscape fabric A synthetic fabric, usually water-permeable, that is spread under paths or mulch to serve as a weed barrier.

Lawn restoration Improving a lawn without killing or removing all of the existing turf.

Lime, limestone A white or grayish mineral compound used to combat soil acidity and to supply calcium for plant growth.

Loam A soil consisting of a mixture of sand, silt, and clay that is ideal for growing.

Mass planting Filling an area with one or a few kinds of plants, such as ground covers, spaced closely together. Often planted to create a bold, dramatic effect or to reduce lawn maintenance.

Microclimate Conditions of sun, shade, exposure, wind, drainage, and other factors that affect plant growth at any particular site.

Mowing strip A row of bricks or paving stones set flush with the soil around the edge of a lawn area and wide enough to support the wheels on one side of a lawn mower.

Mulch A layer of bark, peat moss, compost, shredded leaves, hay or straw, lawn clippings, gravel, paper, plastic, or other material spread over the soil around the base of plants. During the growing season, mulch can help retard evaporation, inhibit weeds, and moderate soil temperature. In the winter, a mulch of evergreen boughs, coarse hay, or leaves is used to protect plants from freezing.

Native A plant that occurs naturally in a particular region and was not introduced from some other area.

Node A joint in grass plants from which leaves emerge.

Nurse grasses Annual grasses used to protect perennial grasses from excess wind and sun while they are becoming established.

Nutrients Nitrogen, phosphorus, potassium, calcium, magnesium, sulfur, iron, and other elements needed by growing plants and supplied by minerals and organic matter in soil and by fertilizers.

Organic matter Plant and animal residues, such as leaves, trimmings, and manure, in various stages of decomposition.

Overseeding Spreading seed over established turf that has been prepared for restoration.

Perennial grasses Grasses that persist year after year, given the right conditions.

Plugs Small round or square pieces of sod that can be planted to establish new lawns.

Pressure-treated lumber Lumber treated with chemicals that protect it from decay.

Rain sensor A device that sends a signal to the automated home sprinkler system's controller that rain is falling so that the controller will turn off and/or delay the restart of sprinklers.

Retaining wall A wall built to stabilize a slope and keep soil from sliding or eroding downhill.

Rhizomes Underground runners of some types of plants that extend laterally to create new plants.

Rotary sprinklers Sprinklers, usually driven by gears, designed to cover large areas. They rotate across a preset arc, such as 90 degrees for placement in a corner, and deliver water in a sweeping motion.

Selective pruning Using pruning shears to remove or cut back the branches of woody plants, usually to give the lawn greater sun exposure.

Sod Carpet-like sheets of turf about ¾ inch thick, 1½ feet wide, and 6 feet long. Strips may be laid over prepared soil to establish new lawns.

Spray sprinklers Sprinklers that produce sprays of various widths without rotation. They have shorter spraying radii than rotary heads and are consequently used for small areas, but they can deliver more gallons per minute.

Sprigs Cut-up lengths of rhizomes or stolons that can be broadcast and pressed into the soil to establish new lawns.

Station A group of sprinkler heads controlled by an automatic valve.

Stolons Aboveground runners from which some grasses, particularly warm-season varieties, spread.

Subsoil A light-colored soil layer usually found beneath the topsoil. It contains little or no humus.

Thatch A mat-like buildup of grass roots and stems (but not of grass blade clippings) that if too thick can inhibit healthy growth.

Tillers Aboveground sideshoots of some types of grass plants. Bunch grasses spread (enlarge) through growth of tillers.

Warm-season grasses Grasses that grow best in southern regions, thriving in the heat of summer.

Watering program The setting of a controller to know what days to water (called watering days), when to water (called a program start time), and how long to water (called station run time).

Weed Any undesirable plant or grass species.

Zone An area of lawn or planting within a landscape that requires similar amounts of water throughout.

INDEX

Pyrethrins, 161
Pythium blight, 149–150

Q
Queen Anne's lace, 164

R
Rakes
  preparing seedbed, 64–65
  types, uses, 108–109
Rakes, power, 111
Renovation of lawn, 44–59
Roller, lawn, 111
  using to prepare soil, 60, 66–67
Rosemary, 164
Rotenone, 161
Rust, 150–151
Ryegrass, perennial, 83

S
Sabadilla, 161–162
Sage, 165
Sedum (stonecrop), 164
Seed
  blends, mixtures, 78
  label information, 78–79
  purchasing, 78
  sowing methods, 60–61
Shade, 37
  reducing by pruning, 131–132
Shovel, round-point, 109
Slit seeder, 111
Slope
  changing to improve drainage, 133
  fixing grade problems, 64
  seeding on, 71
  ways to improve grade, 132–133
Snow drift, minimizing, 26
Sod, 60, 62
  buying tips, 66–67
  laying, 68–69
  preparing soil for, 66–67
Sod cutter, 63, 66–67
Sod webworm, 154–155
Soil
  adding amendments, 36
  composition, ideal, 29–30

compacted, 29–31
erosion, 39
improving, 44
infertile, 32
lack of humus, 33
microbes, 53–54
pH, 36, 50–52
preparing for sod, 65–67
structure, 29
testing, 45–47
type, 28–29
understanding, 46
Solarization, 62
Spade, 109
Spined soldier bugs, 163
Sprayers, 108–109
Spreaders, 51, 53, 108–109
Sprigs, 60–61, 72
Sprinklers
  assessing your system, 123
  automatic in-ground system, 120–123
  head types, 120–121, 123, 125–126
  redesigning, 22–23, 26
  testing system, 115–116
  timers, 115
Square footage, calculating, 116
St. Augustinegrass, 83
Straw-bale compost bin, 33
String trimmer, 110
Stripe smut, 145, 147–148
Stump removal, 132–133
Sulfur
  rates to lower pH, 52
Sun/Shade Log, 37

T
Tansy, 165
Thatch
  causes, 38
  control in lawn, 119
  removing, 38, 48–49, 111, 119
Thyme, 164
Tickseed, 164
Tiller, power, 111
Tools
  hand, 108–109

mowers, types of, 90–93
  renting, 111
Top-dressing with compost, 53–54
Trees
  pruning guidelines, 131
  stump removal, 132–133
Turf
  removing, 62–63
  Turf Condition Score Sheet, 42–43
Turf edger, 63
Typhula blight, 150

V
Vertical mower, 49, 111

W
Walk-behind mower, 101
  buying, 101–105
  maintenance, 106–107
Watering
  amount, 114–116
  frequency, 115–116
  new lawn, 72
  ways to reduce, 114–115
Weeder, 110
Weeds
  annual, 136–137
  cool-season, 136
  control of, 138–141
  cultural measures, 139
  identifying, 136–137
  perennial, 137
  warm-season, 136
Wheelbarrow, 110
White clover, 136
White grubs, 152–153, 156–158

Y
Yard games, space requirements, 21
Yarrow, 165

Z
Zero-turn-radius mower, 92–99
  buying, 94–97
  maintaining, 98–99
Zoysiagrass, 83, 85

PHOTO CREDITS

page 1: Larry Lefever from Grant Heilman Photography, Inc. **page 2:** Home & Garden Editorial Services **page 5:** Home & Garden Editorial Services **page 6:** Larry Lefever/Jane Grushow from Grant Heilman Photography, Inc. **pages 8-9:** Home & Garden Editorial Services; *inset* courtesy of North Wind Picture Archives **page 10:** Home & Garden Editorial Services **page 11:** *top* Barry L. Runk/Stanley Schoenberger from Grant Heilman Photography, Inc.; *bottom* courtesy of North Wind Picture Archives **pages 12-13:** Home & Garden Editorial Services **page 14:** Crandall & Crandall **page 15:** *top* Larry Lefever from Grant Heilman Photography, Inc.; *bottom left* Crandall & Crandall; *bottom right* House & Garden Editorial Services **page 16:** Crandall & Crandall **page 17:** Home & Garden Editorial Services **page 18:** Neil Soderstrom **page 22:** *top* Home & Garden Editorial Services; *bottom* Robert Perron **page 23:** courtesy of The Toro Company **pages 24-25:** Home & Garden Editorial Services **page 26:** Janet Loughrey Photography **page 27:** *top* Larry Lefever/Jane Grushow from Grant Heilman Photography, Inc.; *bottom* Catriona Tudor Erler **page 28:** Barry L. Runk from Grant Heilman Photography, Inc. **page 29:** Home & Garden Editorial Services **page 30:** Home & Garden Editorial Services **page 31:** *top* Neil Soderstrom; *bottom* Home & Garden Editorial Services **page 32:** *top left & top right* Home & Garden Editorial Services; *bottom* Neil Soderstrom **page 33:** Neil Soderstrom **pages 34-35:** Home & Garden Editorial Services **pages 38-39:** Home & Garden Editorial Services **page 40:** *top left & bottom* Dr. Peter Landschoot; *top right* Dr. Ray Kriner from Grant Heilman Photography, Inc. **page 41:** *top* Home & Garden Editorial Services; *bottom* courtesy of The Toro Company **page 42:** Home & Garden Editorial Services **page 43:** Neil Soderstrom **pages 44-45:** Home & Garden Editorial Services **page 47:** Home & Garden Editorial Services **page 48:** Home & Garden Editorial Services **pages 50-51:** Home & Garden Editorial Services **page 53:** Home & Garden Editorial Services **page 55:** Home & Garden Editorial Services **pages 56-57:** Home & Garden Editorial Services **page 58:** Dwight Kuhn **page 59:** courtesy of The Toro Company **page 60:** Home & Garden Editorial Services **page 61:** *top left & bottom left* Karen Williams; *top right & bottom right* Home & Garden Editorial Services **page 62:** Home & Garden Editorial Services **page 63:** *top left, top right, & bottom left* Home & Garden Editorial Services; *bottom right* courtesy of Bluebird International, Inc. **pages**

64-65: Home & Garden Editorial Services **page 67:** Home & Garden Editorial Services **pages 68-69:** Home & Garden Editorial Services **page 70:** *top left & top right* Larry Lefever from Grant Heilman Photography, Inc.; *bottom* Karen Williams **page 71:** Home & Garden Editorial Services **page 72:** Karen Williams **page 73:** Home & Garden Editorial Services **page 76:** Home & Garden Editorial Services **page 77:** courtesy of The Toro Company **page 79:** Home & Garden Editorial Services **page 82:** Dr. Peter Landschoot **page 84:** *top left, middle left, middle right, & bottom right* Dr. Shirley Anderson; *top right* Dr. Peter Landschoot; *bottom left* Karen Williams **page 86:** *top & bottom* Steve Wiest/Jack Fry; *middle* Philip Rosenlund **pages 88-89:** Home & Garden Editorial Services **pages 90-91:** Home & Garden Editorial Services **pages 92-93:** Home & Garden Editorial Services **page 95:** Home & Garden Editorial Services **page 96:** Home & Garden Editorial Services **pages 98-99:** Home & Garden Editorial Services **page 100:** Home & Garden Editorial Services **pages 102-103:** Home & Garden Editorial Services **pages 104-105:** Home & Garden Editorial Services **pages 106-107:** Home & Garden Editorial Services **pages 112-113:** Home & Garden Editorial Services **page 114:** Home & Garden Editorial Services **page 115:** *top & middle* Home & Garden Editorial Services; *bottom* L.R. Nelson **page 116:** Home & Garden Editorial Services **pages 120-121:** courtesy of The Toro Company **page 123:** courtesy of The Toro Company **page 124:** courtesy of The Toro Company **page 126:** courtesy of The Toro Company **page 128:** courtesy of The Scotts Miracle-Gro Company **page 129:** Home & Garden Editorial Services **pages 130-131:** Home & Garden Editorial Services **pages 134-135:** courtesy of The Scotts Miracle-Gro Company **page 136:** courtesy of The Scotts Miracle-Gro Company **page 137:** *top left & top right* courtesy of The Scotts Miracle-Gro Company; *bottom left & bottom right* Home & Garden Editorial Services **page 138:** *top left, bottom left, & bottom right* Home & Garden Editorial Services; *top right* Neil Soderstrom **pages 140-141:** Home & Garden Editorial Services **page 142:** *top left* Dr. Peter Landschoot; *top center* Jim Strawser from Grant Heilman Photography, Inc.; *top right* Home & Garden Editorial Services; *bottom left & bottom center* Barry L. Runk/Stanley Schoenberger from Grant Heilman Photography, Inc.; *bottom right* Neil Soderstrom **page 143:** *top left & bottom right* Rita Buchanan; *top center, top right, & bottom left* Neil Soderstrom; *bottom*

center Jim Strawser from Grant Heilman Photography, Inc. **page 144:** Dr. Peter Landschoot **page 145:** *top* Dr. Peter Landschoot; *middle* Stanley Schoenberger from Grant Heilman Photography, Inc.; *bottom* Barry L. Runk/Stanley Schoenberger from Grant Heilman Photography, Inc. **page 146:** *top* Catriona Tudor Erler; *bottom* Dr. Peter Landschoot **page 147:** Dr. Peter Landschoot **page 148:** Home & Garden Editorial Services **page 149:** *top left* Stanley Schoenberger from Grant Heilman Photography, Inc.; *top center* Barry L. Runk/Stanley Schoenberger from Grant Heilman Photography, Inc.; *top right, bottom left, bottom center, & bottom right* courtesy of American Phytopathological Society **page 151:** *top left* courtesy of The Scotts Miracle-Gro Company; *top right & middle left* Dr. Peter Landschoot; *middle right* Alan and Linda Detrick; *bottom left & bottom right* courtesy of American Phytopathological Society **page 152:** Barry L. Runk/Stanley Schoenberger from Grant Heilman Photography, Inc. **page 153:** John Colwell from Grant Heilman Photography, Inc. **page 154:** Barry L. Runk/Stanley Schoenberger from Grant Heilman Photography, Inc. **page 155:** *top & bottom right* Dwight Kuhn; *bottom left* Grant Heilman Photography, Inc. **page 157:** *top left & top right* Dr. Ray Kriner from Grant Heilman Photography, Inc.; *middle left, bottom left, & bottom right* Barry L. Runk/Stanley Schoenberger from Grant Heilman Photography, Inc.; *middle right* Barry L. Runk from Grant Heilman Photography, Inc. **page 158:** *top left* Barry L. Runk from Grant Heilman Photography, Inc.; *top right* Dwight Kuhn; *bottom left* Jim Strawser from Grant Heilman Photography, Inc.; *bottom right* Grant Heilman Photography, Inc. **page 159:** Home & Garden Editorial Services **page 161:** *top left* Parwinder Grewal; *bottom left* Barry L. Runk/Stanley Schoenberger from Grant Heilman Photography, Inc.; *right* courtesy of Gardens Alive! **page 162:** *top left & bottom right* Barry L. Runk/Stanley Schoenberger from Grant Heilman Photography, Inc.; *top center* James P. Rowan; *top right* Dwight Kuhn; *bottom left & bottom center* Arthur C. Smith from Grant Heilman Photography, Inc. **page 163:** *top* Ken Cole/Animals Animals/Earth Scenes; *bottom* Barry L. Runk/Stanley Schoenberger from Grant Heilman Photography, Inc. **page 164:** *left* Susan A. Roth; *center & right* Neil Soderstrom **page 165:** Neil Soderstrom **page 166:** courtesy of Gardens Alive! **page 167:** Tom "The Moleman" Schmidt **page 169:** Home & Garden Editorial Services

Have a home gardening, decorating, or improvement project? Look for these and other fine Creative Homeowner books wherever books are sold.

An impressive guide to more than 100 flowering plants. More than 500 color photos. 208 pp.; 9" × 10"
BOOK #: 274032

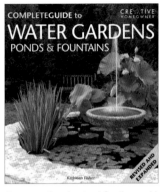

A comprehensive tool for the aspiring water gardener. Over 600 color photos. 240 pp.; 9" × 10"
BOOK #: 274458

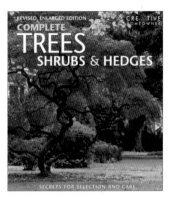

How to select and care for landscaping plants. Over 700 color photos and illustrations. 240 pp.; 9" × 10"
BOOK #: 274222

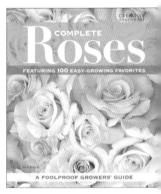

A growing guide for beginners and experienced gardeners. Over 280 color photos. 176 pp.; 9" × 10"
BOOK #: 274061

Guide to creating beautiful gardens. Over 1,000 photos and illustrations. 400 pp.; 9" × 10"
BOOK #: 274021

Inspiring ideas to achieve stunning effects with the landscape. Over 350 photos. 208pp.; 8 1/2" × 10 7/8"
BOOK #: 274154

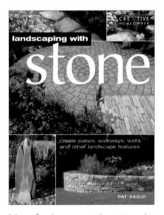

Ideas for incorporating stone into the landscape. Over 400 color photos and illos. 224 pp.; 8 1/2" × 10 7/8"
BOOK #: 274172

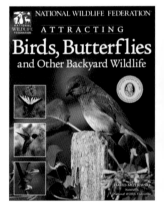

Wildlife-friendly gardening practices and projects. Over 200 color photos and illos. 128 pp.; 8 1/2" × 10 7/8"
BOOK #: 274655

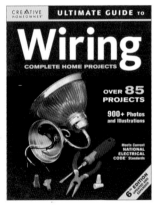

New, updated edition of best-selling house wiring manual. Over 850 color photos. 320 pp.; 8 1/2" × 10 7/8"
BOOK #: 278242

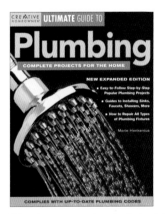

Take the guesswork out of plumbing repair. More than 800 photos and illustrations. 288 pp.; 8 1/2" × 10 7/8"
BOOK #: 278200

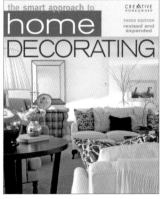

How to work with space, color, pattern, and texture. Over 500 photos. 304 pp.; 9" × 10 7/8"
BOOK #: 279679

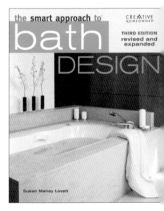

All you need to know about designing a bath. Over 260 color photos. 224 pp.; 9" × 10 7/8"
BOOK #: 279239

For more information, and to place an order, go to **www.creativehomeowner.com**